THE
GOSPEL
OF
JESUS

THE
GOSPEL
OF
JESUS

*In Search of the
Original Good News*

———•◆•———

JAMES M. ROBINSON

HarperSanFrancisco
A Division of HarperCollins*Publishers*

HarperCollins books may be purchased for educational, business, or sales promotional use. For information please write: Special Markets Department, HarperCollins Publishers, 10 East 53rd Street, New York, NY 10022.

HarperCollins Web site: http://www.harpercollins.com
HarperCollins®, ■®, and HarperSanFrancisco™ are
trademarks of HarperCollins Publishers.

FIRST EDITION
Designed by Joseph Rutt

Library of Congress Cataloging-in-Publication Data is available.

ISBN-13: 978–0–06–076217–9
ISBN-10: 0–06–076217–9

05 06 07 08 09 RRD(H) 10 9 8 7 6 5 4 3 2 1

CONTENTS

———◆———

THE FOCUS ON JESUS' GOSPEL

In this Introduction I want to summarize Jesus' gospel, in as clear language as I can, so that no one can miss his point. The rest of the book will spell it all out in more detail; indeed, the Notes contain the scriptural references, so you can look up as much as you like. But I want to put up front the outcome of all that, without any cluttering quotations or digressions, so that you do not lose the point. This book is intended less to provide information about Jesus than it is to let you listen to what he had to say back then, so that you can respond to what he may still have to say today.

The focus of Jesus' gospel was God taking the lead in people's lives, God remaking the world through people who listen to him. Jesus' favorite idiom for God in action was the "kingdom of God." A better translation might be the "reign of God" or "God reigning." This was not a common idiom of his day, to judge by the Jewish texts of his time that have survived, for the idiom is surprisingly rare. Apparently it was Jesus who first made it the central idiom for his message. Since the ideal of God reigning is the main idea Jesus talked about again and again, much of the book focuses on what he meant when he spoke that way.

By using the "kingdom of God," Jesus put his ideal for society in an antithetical relation both to other political and social systems and to individual self-interest ("looking out for number one"). The human dilemma is, in large part, that we are each other's fate. We become the tool of evil that ruins another person as we look out for ourselves, having long abandoned any youthful idealism we might once have cherished. But if we each would cease and desist from pushing the other down to keep ourselves up, then the vicious cycle would be broken. Society would become mutually supportive rather than self-destructive. This is what Jesus was up to.

Jesus' message was simple, for he wanted to cut straight through to the point: trust God to look out for you by providing people who will care for you, and listen to him when he calls on you to provide for them. God is somebody you can trust, so give it a try.

Jesus found his role models for such godly living in the world of nature around him. Ravens and lilies do not seem to focus their attention on satisfying their own needs in order to survive, and yet God sees to it that they prosper. Sparrows are sold a dime a dozen and, one might say, who cares? God cares! Even about the tiniest things—he knows exactly how many hairs are on your head! So God will not give a stone when asked for bread or a snake when asked for fish, but can be counted on to give what you really need. You can trust him to know what you need even before you ask.

This utopian vision of a caring God was the core of what Jesus had to say and what he himself put into practice. It was both good news—reassurance that in your actual experience good would happen to mitigate your plight—and the call upon you to do that same good toward others in actual practice. This radical trust in and responsiveness to God is what makes society function as God's society. This was, for Jesus, what faith and discipleship were all about. As a result, nothing else had a right to claim any functional relationship to him.

Put in language derived from his sayings: I am hungry because you hoard food. You are cold because I hoard clothing. Our dilemma is that we all hoard supplies in our backpacks and put our trust in our wallets! Such "security" should be replaced by God reigning, which means both what I trust God to do (to activate you to share food with me) and what I hear God telling me to do (to share clothes with you). We should not carry money while bypassing the poor or wear a backpack with extra clothes and food while ignoring the cold and hungry lying in the gutter. This is why the beggars, the hungry, the depressed are fortunate: God, that is, those in whom God rules, those who hearken to God, will care for them. The needy are called upon to trust that God's reigning is there for them ("Theirs is the kingdom of God").

We should not even carry a stick for self-protection but, rather, risk doing good for evil, even toward our enemies. We must turn the other cheek! God is the kind of person who provides sunshine and refreshing showers even to those who oppose him. For this reason, God's children are those who care even for their enemies.

What followed directly upon and defined "Thy kingdom come" in the oldest form of the Lord's Prayer used by Jesus was "Give us this day our daily bread." People should pray for a day's ration of food, trusting God to provide for today, and then pray tomorrow, trusting God for tomorrow.

God reigning (the "kingdom of God") was interpreted by Matthew's community to mean: "Thy will be done on earth as it is in heaven." This addition to the Lord's Prayer is, technically speaking, not a call to action, but, like "Thy kingdom come," which it interprets, an appeal to God to act. After all, when we pray, we trust in God to answer. But God answers by motivating

people to turn the other cheek, to give the shirt off their back, to
go the second mile, to lend expecting nothing in return—in sum,
to do God's will on earth. Those who dare to pray to God for
help are the same people whom God motivates to help: "Forgive
us our debts as we forgive our debtors!"

Part of God reigning in Jesus' day was helping the sick, the in-
valids of that day, with whatever medical assistance was available
in Galilee at the time. One went from door to door, and if admitted for what we might call "bed and breakfast" (which was God's
answer to the prayer for a day's bread), one in turn placed God's
blessing on the house by healing as best one could any bedridden
who lived there. Just as the sharing of food and clothing, the canceling of debts, and nonretaliation against enemies were not seen
as human virtues, but rather as God acting through those who
trusted him, just so healings were not attributed to the individual
technique or skill of the healer—but to God acting, reigning,
through Jesus and others.

Clearly all these are things we cannot do by our own strength
and virtue—we are no more up to renouncing self-interest than
we are capable of healing disease! Healings took place because
God was doing the healing. God was reigning in this new kind of
human society Jesus was calling into being—this was in fact the
"coming" of the "kingdom of God": "If it is by the finger of God
that I cast out demons, then there has come upon you God's
reign." Jesus was a "faith healer" in the sense that he trusted God
to thrust his finger into the human dilemma, to relieve the plight
of the physically and mentally ill.

But not everything had been done in the brief time that Jesus
had before his death. Not all people lived such trust in God, not
all the helpless were helped, not all the disabled healed. In fact,
only a few! The disciples trusted God to carry through to completion what was begun in Jesus' time. Theologians use a
pompous term for such hope: "eschatology." But Jesus' message

was not intended to replace the grim reality of daily life with a utopian ideal of "pie in the sky by and by." John the Baptist grimly predicted the end of the world, an "apocalypse," but Jesus did not. Rather, he sought to focus attention on trusting God for today's ration of life, and on hearing God's call to give now a better life to neighbors, indeed to enemies.

All this is as far from today's Christianity as it was from the Judaism of Jesus' day. Christians all too often simply venerate the "Lord Jesus Christ" as the "Son of God" and let it go at that. But Jesus himself made no claim to lofty titles or even to divinity. Indeed, to him, a devout Jew, claiming to be God would have seemed blasphemous! He claimed "only" that God spoke and acted through him.

He insisted that what acquits in the day of judgment is having listened to what he had to say: trust God to care for you, and hear God calling on you to care for your neighbor! What could in substance have shown more esteem on the part of his disciples than committing their destiny to what Jesus had to say to them? Yet the hardest saying of Jesus both then and now is: "Why do you call me 'Master, Master,' and do not do what I say?" Mouthing creeds may be no more than pious dodges to avoid Jesus' unavoidable condition of discipleship—actually to do what he said to do!

People do not do what he said not simply because of the shift in cultural conditions ("times have changed"), but ultimately because people do not trust God as Jesus did (in spite of claims to having Christian faith). This is what is most unsettling about finding out what Jesus had to say—you discover that you do not really want to "walk in his footsteps"! Jesus' gospel sounds incredibly naïve. Once Jesus launched himself into this lifestyle, practicing what he preached, he did not last long. Is not a reality check called for?

Yet the bottom line is not necessarily so cynical. In concentration camps, cells of a few selfless people who could really trust each other, and who were hence willing to give an extra portion of their meager food and other necessities of life to the most needy among them, have turned out to have a better chance of survival than did individuals looking out only for themselves. Selfishness may ultimately turn out to be a luxury we can ill afford. Of course, our plight is not so desperate, and so we do not have to turn to such drastic measures. Think of the rich young ruler, who was just plain too well off, too much like us, to become a disciple of Jesus.

One of Jesus' paradoxical sayings is: "When you save your life you lose it, but when you lose your life you save it." To be sure, the point of this saying is not longevity, but integrity. But what Jesus had to say is all the more worthy of serious consideration.

Jesus' cause in life was not improving fishing conditions on the Sea of Galilee, evading Roman taxation, avoiding gentile pollution, or many other issues he knew about as a Galilean Jew, all of which are not our issues today. Nor did his message consist of the trivia typical of holy men of the day, irrelevant to us today, such as healing techniques that no physician would dare prescribe, magic formulas to cast out nonexistent demons, predictions as to when the world would come to an end, or even how to get rid of the Romans and restore Israel's own kingdom. Rather, he grappled with the basic issues of human existence, which have not changed and with which each generation, each culture, including ours, has to grapple. Jesus was a profound person who found a solution to the human dilemma, which he implemented in his own life and urged anyone who would listen to implement.

It is human nature to need food, clothing, and protection from the elements; to have to cope somehow with infancy, pain, sickness, and senility; to fulfill sexual needs, have a family, and work for its survival; and to search for some sense in it all. These are things we know about firsthand, since we ourselves have to grapple with these same basic ingredients of being human. How others have grappled and what solutions they have found is an unavoidable interest we all share. We imitate or react against our parents and other role models. We look up to persons we consider "great," precisely because of the way they resolved these basic human needs.

The way Jesus reached a basic understanding of the human dilemma and proposed a solution was of course couched in the language and options of his cultural situation, which is not ours. But the dilemma he confronted is still our dilemma, even though we have to recast it in new language and modern alternatives. The problem inherent in understanding the gospel of Jesus is to translate it from his cultural situation into ours, his specifics into ours, his language into ours. This applies both to the forms that the human dilemma took in his situation and takes in ours, and to the solution he offered in his and our translation of that into ours. Only in this way are we able really to listen to him and think through for ourselves what he had to say.

His basic issue, still basic today, is that most people have solved the human dilemma for themselves at the expense of everyone else, putting them down so as to stay afloat themselves. This vicious, antisocial way of coping with the necessities of life only escalates the dilemma for the rest of society. All of us know the result all too well, for we have experienced it ourselves in one form or another: the breakdown of mutually supportive human relations that results in the distinction between the haves and have-nots; the ruling class subjugating serfs, sharecroppers, and blue-collar workers; the battle of the sexes; dictatorships of one kind or the other; exploitation in the workplace; and on and on.

Jesus came to grips with the basic intentions of people. He addressed them personally, as to what kind of people they were. He called on them—he did not just teach them ideas. When we take his sayings and distill from them our doctrines, what we have really done is manipulate his sayings for our own purposes, first of all, for the purpose of avoiding his personal address to us. Without realizing it, we reclassify his sayings as objective teachings to which we can give intellectual assent, rather than letting them strike home as the personal challenge he intended them to be. The issue is not what we think about them, but rather what we do about them.

So the very objectivity of a scholar would really be—a dodge, a way to avoid Jesus' point! So if I, near the end of my scholarly career, am really going to try to talk about what he had to say, I have to try to talk more in the way he talked—I have to retain his note of direct appeal. This tone of encounter, this person-to-person mode, is the only really objective way to speak to you about what Jesus was talking about, for it was that personal talk that he was talking and walking.

Jesus deserves more than being shelved as nothing more than a lofty curiosity in our cultural heritage. He needs to be taken seriously, really to be heard. In the chapters that follow, specifics of his biography, lifestyle, convictions, program, and outcome will be analyzed in just such an effort to take him seriously enough to hear what he had to say then, and still has to say today.

This is not just another book about Jesus; it is a book about the gospel of Jesus.

THE
GOSPEL
OF
JESUS

———•◆•———

ONE

THE LOST GOSPEL
OF JESUS

The rash title of this book, *The Gospel of Jesus*, does not have in view the gospel about Jesus that Paul preached, which, following him, the Christian church down through the ages has believed as the one and only gospel (see Chapter 10). Rather, the title refers to the gospel that was Jesus' own message in Galilee during a very brief period, probably no more than a year, before his crucifixion. These two gospels are not the same, and, what is even worse, Jesus' own gospel has been lost from sight, hidden behind the gospel of the church.

This little book certainly does not tell everything you would like to know about Jesus. It does not even tell everything that *can* be known about him. It is not intended to satisfy your curiosity about odds and ends, but to focus on what Jesus was up to. So it does contain the core, what Jesus considered his own gospel.

Whatever might be added that would distract from that focus would not be faithful to Jesus, no matter how factual it might be. You also may not find here your "favorite" material of Jesus', which may well be unconsciously preferred precisely because it has been domesticated, watered down, or even just put on Jesus' lips, rather than being what was central to him, what he himself had to say. Listening to Jesus is not easy.

The disciples handed down sayings and stories that meant something to them, not just stray information that satisfied their curiosity. They stuck to what they considered basics.

Our real problem with Jesus is not the vast amount of detail we will never know, for most of that we do not need to know. The problem is that we have ascribed to him a different gospel from what he himself envisaged! We have put him on a pedestal and worshiped him, rather than walking in his footsteps. Put somewhat differently: we must work our way back through the church's own familiar gospel and its domestication of the gospel of Jesus. Only then do we strike upon what he really had to say, which was a brittle, upsetting, comforting, challenging gospel— one the present book seeks to lay bare.

This situation calls for some explanation, before we turn to his message itself.

THE APOSTLES' CREED

The Apostles' Creed, shared among almost all branches of Christianity, poses the problem clearly, even if unintentionally. It presents Jesus as the central figure in the Trinity in heaven, rather than as the individual he was in Galilee. Listen closely to the way the creed presents him. Before reporting that Jesus went to heaven, the creed only tells what was done *for* him:

conceived by the Holy Ghost, born of the Virgin Mary

and then what was done *against* him:

suffered under Pontius Pilate, was crucified, dead, and buried

But on his life between birth and death, Bethlehem and Golgotha, the creed is completely silent! Missing is what was said and done *by* Jesus, what Jesus himself actually had to say by way of gospel.

The present book seeks to fill in the missing gospel of that Galilean Jesus. It is he, even more than Mary, and surely more than Pontius Pilate, who is the central person in the Apostles' Creed, even if, so to speak, in absentia.

The name "Apostles' Creed" is itself a misnomer, if it is taken to mean that it was composed by the twelve apostles, indeed by any of Jesus' Galilean followers. It actually developed out of the baptismal confession of the gentile church of Rome, documented only from the second century on. How the original disciples themselves would have put it can be inferred only by going back through the Gospels to the oldest traditions they preserve—which is precisely what I propose to do here.

THE SAYINGS GOSPEL Q

The primary source for knowing Jesus is to be found in the pithy and memorable sayings he used to move his listeners to trust in God enough to go into action. They are what lived on after him, they are what his disciples continued to proclaim—in spite of experiencing his utterly appalling execution (see Chapter 9). You might think the crucifixion would have crushed their faith in all that Jesus had said and silenced even their best intentions. But their experience of Jesus still calling on them to continue his message and lifestyle was the substance of the resurrection experience.

It was his sayings that kept alive stories about what Jesus had done, indeed engendered more and more stories about him. These oral traditions moved from Aramaic into the more literate Greek and came to be written into Gospels, which were ultimately preserved. They were included in the New Testament, which was established in the next centuries as the "canon," that is, as the standard for all that is to be considered Christian.

To gain admission to the canon, Gospels were attributed to apostles (Matthew and John) or to those dependent on apostles for their information (Mark and Luke). But today, these persons are not thought to have been the actual authors. None of the texts themselves give the author's name—all four are anonymous. They were composed in the last thirty years of the first century, half a century after the facts. Their actual authors are unknown, but all four Gospels are of course cited here by their traditional names, Matthew, Mark, Luke, and John.

In modern times, the quest of the historical Jesus has sought to bring to the surface the Galilean Jesus behind the Gospels. This quest began in the nineteenth century with the rise of modern historical scholarship. First of all, it was noted that the narratives of Matthew, Mark, and Luke contain many of the same stories in much the same sequence, whereas the Gospel of John goes its own way. Indeed, the Gospel of John is the latest of the four, from the last decade of the first century, and reflects more of the church's gospel about Jesus than it does the gospel of Jesus himself. It is the most important Gospel for the history of theology, but the least important for the quest of the historical Jesus.

As a result, the first three Gospels came to be called the "synoptic" Gospels, since they see Jesus from the same point of view. The "synoptic problem" has traditionally been the attempt to explain this similarity of Matthew, Mark, and Luke to each other over against John. The solution found almost two centuries ago was that the Gospels of Matthew and Luke used most of the Gospel of Mark, which is thus the oldest Gospel. Since it seems to refer to the fall of Jerusalem,[1] it probably was written shortly after 70 C.E., when the Romans destroyed the temple and the city.

This generally accepted solution to the synoptic problem left one issue dangling, however. Many sayings in Matthew and Luke are much the same in wording and order in both Gospels—but these shared sayings cannot be explained as derived from Mark, since they are not to be found there. You can check this out for yourself by looking up the very beginning of Jesus' public ministry: the sayings of John the Baptist,[2] followed by the temptations of Jesus,[3] and then the opening "Sermon"—located "on the Mount" in Matthew[4] and "on the Plain" in Luke[5]—all absent from Mark and yet shared by Matthew and Luke.

How then did Matthew and Luke come by this shared material, mostly sayings, that cannot have come from Mark, since it is not in Mark? The most widely held solution, launched already in 1838, is that Matthew and Luke shared a second source, like Mark written in Greek, consisting almost exclusively of sayings rather than narratives. For lack of a better name, this collection of sayings came to be referred to simply as Matthew and Luke's other "source," in German *Quelle,* from which the initial "Q" was lifted up as the "title." It was really only a nickname, but it has stuck.

Then another Gospel consisting only of sayings, the *Gospel of Thomas,* turned up in a manuscript discovery of 1945, the Nag Hammadi Codices.[6] This discovery was a collection of thirteen books buried near Nag Hammadi in Upper (that is to say, southern) Egypt in the last half of the fourth century. We call them "codices," to distinguish them from scrolls, since they were like modern books with pages that can be turned, rather than rolls that can be unwound. That is to say, each is a "codex."

The Nag Hammadi Codices consist of a collection of almost fifty offbeat Christian texts, called tractates. All were originally composed in Greek at various locations in the eastern Mediterranean world, but the copies that survived in Egypt are all in Coptic translation. Coptic is actually Egypt's ancient pharaonic language, which in early Christian times was written with Greek letters, since hieroglyphs had long since died out.

After the discovery of the complete text of the *Gospel of Thomas* in Coptic translation, scholars realized that fragments of three copies of the Greek text itself had been discovered half a century earlier at Oxyrhynchus in Upper Egypt.[7] They are more than a century older than the Nag Hammadi Codices, but in most cases are too fragmentary to be of much use.

Clearly, Gospels were not always narratives of Jesus' life; some were just collections of his sayings, such as Q and the *Gospel of Thomas.* Of late, such collections of sayings have come to be called "sayings Gospels," to distinguish them from the "narrative Gospels" with which we have long been familiar from the New Testament. The sayings collection used by Matthew and Luke is no longer known only by its nickname, Q, but has finally been given its own name, the Sayings Gospel Q.

This rediscovered Sayings Gospel Q is not readily available to the public, since it is not as such in the Bible; it has to be reconstructed from the tradition behind the shared sayings in the Gospels of Matthew and Luke. For this reason my translation of the Sayings Gospel Q is included for convenience in the present volume (see Chapter 2).

In order to understand why there were originally two, Mark and Q, rather than just one oldest Gospel, we need to recall that from very early on there were two "denominations" in Christianity—each with its own Gospel. The success of the gentile mission of Paul and Barnabas had resulted in the decision at the Jerusalem Council, held around 50 C.E., to admit uncircumcised gentile converts to Christianity. But to avoid mixing Christian Gentiles with Christian Jews, which would make the Christian Jews ceremonially impure in Jewish terms, the Christian Gentiles were to form a separate branch of Christianity. This gentile church wrote up its traditions about Jesus and thus produced the Gospel of Mark as its Gospel.

One indication that the Gospel of Mark was written for the gentile church is that Mark, rather than postponing the expansion of the Christian mission to include Gentiles until after the resurrection, as Matthew does with the "great commission," has an equivalent sanctioning of the gentile mission prior to the crucifixion:

And the good news must first be proclaimed to all nations.[8]

That Mark was written for Gentiles is seen most clearly in his explanation of Jewish customs for his gentile readers:

For the Pharisees, and all the Jews, do not eat unless they thoroughly wash their hands, thus observing the tradition of the elders; and they do not eat anything from the market unless they wash it; and there are also many other traditions that they observe, the washing of cups, pots, and bronze kettles.[9]

Mark is also writing for a community that is no longer fully bilingual, for he translates Aramaic and Hebrew expressions into Greek for his Greek-only readers:

He took her by the hand and said to her, "*Talitha cum,*" which means, "Little girl, get up!"

Then looking up to heaven, he sighed and said to him, "*Ephphatha,*" that is, "Be opened."

"*Eloi, eloi, lema sabachthani?*" which means, "O my God, o my God, why have you abandoned me?"[10]

In addition, Mark does not seem to know Palestinian geography very well, which may suggest he is not from that region:

> Then he returned from the region of Tyre, and went by way of Sidon towards the Sea of Galilee, in the region of the Decapolis.[11]

Tyre and Sidon are both on the Mediterranean northwest of the Sea of Galilee, but Tyre is much to the south of Sidon. One would not go through Sidon when going south from Tyre. And the Decapolis is well inland, southeast of the Sea of Galilee; one would not pass through it on the way from the Mediterranean to the Sea of Galilee. So this itinerary reads as if Mark did not have a much clearer picture of the geography of the region than do most of us.

On the other hand, the Jewish church was made up of the immediate disciples of Jesus, all of whom were Jews, who after Jesus' death resumed preaching his sayings. The result was that small collections of his sayings were brought together for preaching purposes and in the process translated from Aramaic into Greek. These small collections were over a period of time supplemented with new material, and the whole was edited around the year 70, at about the time of the Jewish war, thus finally producing the Sayings Gospel Q.

Just as there are indications in the Gospel of Mark that it was written for a gentile Christian audience, there are indications in the Sayings Gospel Q that it was written for a Jewish Christian audience. It includes derogatory statements about Gentiles like those that were no doubt common in the Aramaic-speaking Jewish villages:

> And if you lend to those from whom you hope to receive, what reward do you have? Do not even the Gentiles do the same?

So why be anxious, saying: "What are we to eat?" Or: "What are we to drink?" Or: "What are we to wear?" For all these the Gentiles seek; for your Father knows that you need them all.[12]

The Jewish Christian church finally merged with the gentile Christian church. No doubt as an ecumenical gesture, it blended the Gospels of each branch of Christianity, Q and Mark, to produce the Gospel of Matthew. Similarly the gentile Christian church blended the same two original Gospels into its Gospel of Luke. But its Evangelist included a second volume, the Acts of the Apostles, narrating the success of the gentile mission. This is why we know so much more about the gentile church than about the Jewish church in this early period. When in the second and subsequent centuries the gentile Christian church collected its authoritative writings into what became the New Testament, it included its oldest Gospel, Mark, but did not include the oldest Gospel of the Jewish Christian denomination, the Sayings Gospel Q.

It is because Q and Mark are one stage behind Matthew and Luke, one stage nearer to Jesus, that they, rather than Matthew and Luke, are usually quoted in what follows. Only when something distinctive of Matthew or Luke is relevant are they cited. Since the reconstructed Sayings Gospel Q is the best source that exists today to get back to what Jesus actually had to say, it is also the best source for understanding what he thought he was doing, what he was up to in what he did.

The narrative Gospels do not seem to have been composed in a community of persons who actually heard Jesus speak. But of course they do have information not found elsewhere, information that is important and should not be lost from sight. But the sayings of the Sayings Gospel Q—of course not all of them, but the oldest layer—do go back to the community of those who had heard and remembered what Jesus had said. Indeed, they preserved them not just as nostalgic memories of a past leader, but rather as the true message that they continued to announce in Jesus' name. Many of them are pithy sayings, like one-liners that are not easily forgotten. They made their point when Jesus said them, and when his disciples repeated them in his name. And they can make that same point when we hear them today. The Sayings Gospel Q is thus the primary source for the gospel of Jesus.

WHAT JESUS DID ACCORDING TO Q

Of course you are interested in knowing about what Jesus did, not just what he said. But the Sayings Gospel Q presents him as a person who does precisely the kinds of things the narrative Gospels report (as will be explained in more detail in the rest of the present book; see especially Chapters 6 and 7).

The Sayings Gospel Q makes Jesus' role as faith healer clear in the narration of the healing of the centurion's boy[13] and his role as exorcist clear in the exorcism initiating the Beelzebul controversy.[14] Indeed, the Sayings Gospel Q launched the proof that Jesus was the "one to come" that John had predicted by calling on John's disciples to see and hear what Jesus was *doing*. The Sayings Gospel Q even provided the list of things that Jesus had done that proved it,[15] a list so extensive that Matthew had difficulty documenting it (see Chapter 5).

It is odd that a sayings Gospel would list, as its evidence of who Jesus was, first his healings, before mentioning what he said. Furthermore, the Sayings Gospel Q reports that "mighty works" were performed in Chorazin and Bethsaida.[16] The "mission instructions" in the Sayings Gospel Q also call on the disciples to heal the sick,[17] making clear that Jesus' healing power was carried over to them. Thus Jesus' role as faith healer and exorcist is as clear in the Sayings Gospel Q as it is in the narrative Gospels, even though almost all the healing stories are reserved for the narrative Gospels.

Even more important, it is the Jesus of the Sayings Gospel Q who gave his explanation for the faith healings and exorcisms. So if you wonder what Jesus was really up to in his healings, read the Sayings Gospel Q—it is God reigning!

When Jesus' disciples receive hospitality in a home, he told them:

> Cure the sick there, and say to them: "God's reign has reached unto you."[18]

The exorcisms are similarly explained:

> But if it is by the finger of God that I cast out demons, then there has come upon you God's reign.[19]

The disciples had that same faith that God is reigning; indeed, they were still proclaiming Jesus' message even after his death. So they told the miraculous healing stories with which we are familiar from the narrative Gospels. Indeed, they sometimes used incredibly miraculous language.

For modern people, who have trouble understanding the point of such excessive miracle stories, it is not enough to say that you do not have to take them literally, for then how do you take them? A responsible answer would be: take them the way Jesus in the Sayings Gospel Q says to take them! It is the Sayings Gospel Q that provides the interpretation for such things in the narrative Gospels as faith healings and exorcisms as God's reign taking place (see Chapters 6 and 7). Hence the relevance of the Sayings Gospel Q for understanding Jesus' Galilean ministry as portrayed in the narrative Gospels, and indeed for understanding how and why it actually took place during Jesus' lifetime, can hardly be overestimated.

Not only are stories presenting Jesus as faith healer and as exorcist prominent in the narrative Gospels; so are dramatic scenes presenting him as providing food for hungry masses. Yet it is especially in the Sayings Gospel Q that the actual point of such feeding stories is made clear. The Sayings Gospel Q reports that Jesus explicitly says again and again that you are to count on God to feed the hungry. In the Lord's Prayer, the petition "Let your reign come" is followed directly by what that means in the here and now: "Our day's bread give us today."[20] Jesus promises people that they can trust God for food,[21] for just as God feeds the ravens, just so he feeds humans.[22] Similarly, the worker is assured of receiving food in the mission instructions.[23] Thus, according to the Jesus of the Sayings Gospel Q, food, just like healings, is again and again what happens when God reigns.

Jesus does not exemplify an ascetic way of life, admired though that was in antiquity and exemplified as it was by his mentor, John the Baptist. Rather, he is a person who both eats and shares food with others.[24] This open table fellowship could lead people to imagine him—or, as he would put it, God—feeding people by the thousands.[25]

Of course there is no final proof that even the oldest layer of sayings attributed to Jesus does in fact go back to him. His disciples, in continuing his message after his death, inevitably repeated them in such a way as to avoid misunderstandings that may have arisen and to make clear what they were sure was Jesus' intent by clarifying his wording. But it has become possible to a very large extent to detect such "improvements" and hence to get behind them to the earlier formulation. This oldest layer can be trusted to give an accurate image of what Jesus was up to, what his gospel really was.

Jesus must have spoken Aramaic, his mother tongue (see Chapter 3), whereas we have what he said only in Greek translation, on which our English translations are based. So it is not a matter of verbatim quotations, but of ancient Greek and modern English translations. But they can convey accurately what he had to say.

Readers of the narrative Gospels, and even of the Sayings Gospel Q, must avoid both extremes—being too credulous or too skeptical—in assessing the reliability of the sayings ascribed to Jesus. Later reformulations or even new sayings put on Jesus' tongue should not be ascribed to him, even though they may well be our favorite sayings (see Chapter 8). But the oldest layer of sayings ascribed to him should not be considered unreliable; it should in fact be what we use to talk about Jesus. Otherwise Jesus quite unnecessarily disappears from the pages of history, or "Jesus" becomes an empty category into which wild fantasies can be poured.

FROM THE JESUS OF
THE SAYINGS GOSPEL Q TO US

If the Sayings Gospel Q gives us insight into the thinking and doing of Jesus, how does that connect to us? The Sayings Gospel Q as a document ceased to exist after the first century, when the enlarged and improved editions of Matthew and Luke replaced it for reading in the church. And, since no Christian manuscripts dating back to the first century have survived, no copies of Q survived. The Sayings Gospel Q has been lost for a very long time!

Is not its Jesus, the real Jesus, also gone? Simply detecting, a century and a half ago, a collection of his sayings embedded in Matthew and Luke does not necessarily mean that we have any connection with the real Jesus whose sayings it contains.

The real Jesus was not only in his way otherworldly—he was worlds apart from us! We may still want to understand ourselves as his disciples and his church, to consider him as our Lord—but that is far from obvious. We, the gentile church, are the result of Paul's gentile mission, not of the Sayings Gospel Q's Jewish mission. Paul did not see or hear Jesus during his public ministry in

Galilee, but first encountered Jesus after the crucifixion as a blinding light that spoke to him on the road to Damascus—and who literally and figuratively so outshone the Galilean Jesus as to leave that Jesus out of sight.

What we know about the people behind Q is very limited and must be largely inferred from Q itself, since it has not been recorded elsewhere. What we know about the first generation of Christianity comes either from Paul's Letters or the book of Acts. But Acts is the second volume of the two-volume work Luke-Acts, which presents the foundations of the gentile Christian church. Of course the Gospel of Luke does present Jesus' public ministry in Galilee and then the first chapters of Acts do describe the Jerusalem church, but just in order to have them validate Paul's gentile church.[26] The rest of Acts is the success story of Paul's gentile mission.

Luke-Acts seems quite consciously to be playing down the Jewish Christian Q movement. Once Luke completes his copying out of the Sayings Gospel Q into his narrative Gospel,[27] he rather explicitly says that the idyllic, unreal world of Jesus has been put behind us. That idyllic world had begun with Jesus' successful resistance to the temptations:

> When the devil had finished every temptation, he departed from him until an opportune time.[28]

But the devil returns with a vengeance just in time for the passion narrative:

> Then Satan entered into Judas called Iscariot, who was one of the twelve.

> Simon, Simon, listen! Satan has demanded to sift all of you like wheat.[29]

Luke, having reached the conclusion of the Sayings Gospel Q, turned to the Gospel of Mark for the rest of Jesus' public ministry. Thus Luke has in effect turned from the unreal world free from the grip of the devil back to the real world around him:

> And he said to them, "When I sent you out with no purse or bag or sandals, did you lack anything?" They said, "Nothing." He said to them, "But now, let him who has a purse take it, and likewise a bag. And let him who has no sword sell his mantle and buy one. For I tell you that this scripture must be fulfilled in me, 'And he was reckoned with transgressors'; for what is written about me has its fulfillment." And they said, "Look, Lord, here are two swords." And he said to them, "It is enough."[30]

The disciples must now come to grips with reality, even buy a sword, which meant replacing the kind of mission Jesus had advocated and practiced with one more like the missionary journeys of Paul.

The need for a sword appears at this juncture because Luke is turning to Mark's narration of Jesus' arrest in the garden of Gethsemane, where Jesus is confronted by "a crowd with swords and clubs."[31] A disciple feels called upon to come to his defense:

> But one of those who stood near drew his sword and struck the slave of the high priest, cutting off his ear.[32]

Thus was born the church militant. But Jesus' instructions to the Q community had been not even to carry a stick in self-defense![33]

The continuation of Jesus' ministry by the Q community is not visible in Acts, which focuses instead on the gentile mission led by Paul:

> But you will receive power when the Holy Spirit has come upon you; and you will be my witnesses in Jerusalem, in all Judea and Samaria, and to the ends of the earth.[34]

And Galilee? There is only one single passing reference in all of Acts to there being a church also in Galilee:

> Meanwhile the church throughout Judea, Galilee, and Samaria had peace and was built up.[35]

The author of Luke-Acts of course knew all the sayings of Jesus found in Q and Mark, since he had written with their help the Gospel of Luke. But in reading the book of Acts, one would never imagine that there were still Christians whose religious experience consisted largely in listening to what Jesus had had to say back then.

At the Jerusalem Council, a practical working arrangement of two separate missions had been agreed on:

> . . . agreeing that we should go to the Gentiles while they went to the Jews.[36]

Clearly, Luke in the book of Acts is interested in the kind of religious experience characteristic of the gentile mission, which obviously did not build to any great extent on the sayings of Jesus. So the course of the Q community has to be postulated largely on the basis of Q itself. This is far from ideal, but for the moment it is all we have to go on.

The most obvious thing that can be said about the Q community after it resumed Jesus' message is that it did not meet with much success. Listen to passages in Q that talk of rejection, passages that probably would not have been retained if things had developed quite positively:

To what am I to compare this generation and what is it like? It is like children seated in the marketplaces, who, addressing the others, say: "We fluted for you, but you would not dance; we wailed, but you would not cry." For John came, neither eating nor drinking, and you say: "He has a demon!" The son of man came, eating and drinking, and you say: "Look! A person who is a glutton and drunkard, a chum of tax collectors and sinners!"

But into whatever town you enter and they do not take you in, on going out from that town, shake off the dust from your feet. I tell you: For Sodom it shall be more bearable on that day than for that town. Woe to you, Chorazin! Woe to you, Bethsaida! For if the wonders performed in you had taken place in Tyre and Sidon, they would have repented long ago, in sackcloth and ashes. Yet for Tyre and Sidon it shall be more bearable at the judgment than for you. And for you, Capernaum, up to heaven will you be exalted? Into Hades shall you come down!

This generation is an evil generation; it demands a sign, but a sign will not be given to it—except the sign of Jonah! For as Jonah became to the Ninevites a sign, so also will the son of humanity be to this generation.[37]

The Jewish mission seems to have continued to have little success in the generation after Jesus' own ministry, so that "this generation" was apparently meant rather literally, for the destruction of Jerusalem in the year 70 was taken to be God's punishment for the rejection of the Jewish mission:

O Jerusalem, Jerusalem, who kills the prophets and stones those sent to her! How often I wanted to gather your children

together, as a hen gathers her nestlings under her wings, and
you were not willing! Look, your House is forsaken! I tell you:
You will not see me until the time comes when you say:
"Blessed is the one who comes in the name of the Lord!"[38]

After the Roman armies had marched through Galilee and Judea
and destroyed the temple in Jerusalem, Judaism was of course in
terrible disarray. The very question of its survival was at stake.
The Q community, as a part of the Judaism of the day, was caught
up in this dilemma.

It had always been obvious that those whose temple was the
temple in Jerusalem were Jews, the others Gentiles. To this extent, it was quite clear who was a Jew. This made it possible for
the Jews to have among them various parties that all too readily
rejected each other on other issues, such as the Pharisees, the
Sadducees, the Essenes, the Zealots, the Therapeutae of Alexandria, the Sethians, and then the Christian Jews. But when the
temple that they all claimed was destroyed, where was the Jewish
identity? The plurality of parties was simply a luxury they could
no longer afford. Whatever was left of Judaism had to stand together! The Jewish leaders came together and merged all these
parties into a unified Judaism, which soon became the rabbinic
Judaism out of which modern Judaism emerged. As a result, these
individual groups disappeared from history, among them the
Christian Jews who had composed the Sayings Gospel Q.

Some of the Q community may, like those in the other Jewish
parties, have simply merged into the more unified Judaism, what
came to be called "normative Judaism." Thus they would have
ceased to be identified as Christian. But some apparently per-
sisted in their Christian identity while continuing their Jewish
way of life. These, in turn, came to be rejected by mainline (gentile) Christianity and ended up in lists of heretics.

One such group of "heretics" were the Ebionites, an Aramaic word that means "the poor." Their "heresy" was that they insisted on continuing their Jewish lifestyle. Actually, "the poor" was a very early name for Jesus' followers. There is a real irony in the fact that this "heretical" group bears the same name that was used for the original Christians of Jerusalem,[39] indeed was used by the Q community of itself. It is no coincidence that the first and most important collection of Jesus' sayings in Q, which grew to become the Sermon on the Mount, begins with a blessing on "the poor"[40] and a flashback in Q to this earliest collection refers to Jesus "evangelizing the poor."[41]

At the very earliest time the term "Christian" had not yet been coined. It was first used of Barnabas and Paul's gentile church in Antioch[42] and may never have been used of Jewish Christian groups. As a matter of fact, it may be something of a misnomer when, for simplicity's sake, I refer to the Q community as "Christian."

Another such "heretical" group was called the Nazarenes. This term had also been, from early on, a designation for Jesus himself[43] and even for Paul.[44] But this group maintained the Jewish way of life and so came to be rejected by gentile Christianity.

Once a Jewish Christian group had been rejected by gentile Christianity as heretical, it faded from the pages of history. Fortunately, the Jewish Christian Sayings Gospel Q did not fade from history along with the community whose Gospel it was. Rather, it survived in the gentile church's Gospels of Matthew and Luke.

The Matthean community had originally been confined to Jewish territory, since it maintained prohibitions against using gentile roads and visiting Samaritan towns:

Do not go away on a road of the Gentiles, and enter no town of the Samaritans, but go rather to the lost sheep of the house of Israel.

When they persecute you in one town, flee to the next; for truly I tell you, you will not have gone through all the towns of Israel before the son of man comes.[45]

It is not clear whether these texts were in the Sayings Gospel Q itself, since they are not in Luke; but then Luke would have had every reason to leave them out, for he played up the Samaritan mission in Acts[46] and of course Paul went to the Gentiles. In any case, at some stage in the evolution of the Q community into the Matthean community, this geographical limitation was in effect. But later it would seem to have been suspended, perhaps as a result of the chaos left in the wake of the Roman army's destruction of much of Galilee on its triumphal march toward Jerusalem. The "great commission" with which the Gospel of Matthew concludes explicitly instructs the mission to go to the Gentiles—while emphasizing, not unintentionally, that it is the message of the Sayings Gospel Q that is to be carried on that mission:

All authority in heaven and on earth has been given to me. Go therefore and make disciples of all nations, baptizing them in the name of the Father and of the Son and of the Holy Spirit, and teaching them to observe everything that I have commanded you [!]. And remember, I am with you always, to the end of the age.[47]

Within the Greek text of the Sayings Gospel Q can be seen smaller and larger clusters of individual sayings, which were then finally united into the Sayings Gospel Q as we know it from Matthew and Luke. The most prominent such cluster is what is called the Sermon, though that is really a misnomer, since it is not assumed to be a speech Jesus made on a given occasion. Rather, it is an early collection of Jesus' sayings into what was no doubt considered to be the core of his message. This "sermon" was put at the beginning of Jesus' message in the Sayings Gospel Q. As Matthew and Luke borrowed from Mark, they each fitted the Sermon into Mark at a slightly different geographical location. The result is that in Matthew it is called the Sermon on the Mount[48] and in Luke the Sermon on the Plain.[49]

Matthew enlarged the Sermon by including in it the most important other old clusters, such as the Lord's Prayer,[50] followed by the certainty of the answer of prayer,[51] and the role model of the ravens and lilies.[52] Thus down through the centuries, when the Sayings Gospel Q was completely lost, indeed its very existence unknown, it is the Sermon on the Mount that functioned indirectly to keep its message—the gospel of Jesus—alive.

In the early church, it was thanks to the Gospel of Matthew that the Sayings Gospel Q continued to play a role, if only indirectly. Matthew was by far the most widely used early Christian book, to judge by the number of copies that have surfaced in the dry sands of Egypt, by the number of quotations in early Christian writers, and by the number of textual corruptions introduced from Matthew into other Gospels by scribal copyists obviously more familiar with Matthew.

Paul's Letters were of course the most popular among theologians, but it is not they who converted the Roman Empire. Rather, it was the masses, from whom the foot soldiers in Constantine's army came. They knew firsthand of the underprivileged and oppressed who had been rescued by the soup kitchens (which served more than wafers), the adoption of orphans, the absorption of widows, and the many other forms of humaneness that derive ultimately from Jesus, mediated through the Sayings Gospel Q and then through the Sermon on the Mount. So it was his foot soldiers that the emperor told of having seen the cross in the sky with the message "In this sign conquer!" The troops, heavily Christian and hence pacifistic, fell into line and marched into battle, on to victory.

It seems to have been Francis of Assisi who then rediscovered the Sermon on the Mount. The Franciscan order that emerged from his leadership has been the bearer down through the centuries of much of the message of Jesus found in the Sayings Gospel Q. Then Leo Tolstoy took up the torch in his *War and Peace,* followed by Mahatma Gandhi with his "passive resistance" and Martin Luther King Jr. with his "dream" of an integrated America. Now that the Sayings Gospel Q is readily available for study, we can see how Jesus' message has indeed continued to be heard, though in quite unusual ways, down through the centuries.

TWO

THE SAYINGS
GOSPEL Q

Beginning in 1983, I organized a team of scholars, called the International Q Project, to reconstruct the Sayings Gospel Q word by word. The result of a generation of teamwork by more than forty scholars is available in the rather massive *The Critical Edition of Q* (Leuven: Peeters; Minneapolis: Fortress, 2000). It is more accessible in the abridged edition, *The Sayings Gospel Q in Greek and English* (Leuven: Peeters, 2001; Minneapolis: Fortress, 2002). My resultant English translation of Q is reprinted below.

Anyone wishing to investigate my own research over the past forty years that led up to and accompanied this reconstruction of the text of the Sayings Gospel Q may consult my large volume *The Sayings Gospel Q: Collected Essays* (Leuven: Peeters, 2005), although that volume may be too technical to interest average readers.

In the reconstruction process, the wording of the Sayings Gospel Q had to be worked out in a painstaking word-by-word analysis, saying after saying, to detect and undo the varying stylistic and theological "improvements" that are characteristic of both Matthew and Luke. Since the Gospel of Matthew was rooted in the Q community, it often continued Q's language more faithfully than did the gentile Christian Gospel of Luke. But since the Gospel of Luke did not come from a congregation still making use of the Sayings Gospel Q, it had less need to update the Q text and hence often has the older reading. The Sayings Gospel Q itself is not in the New Testament, but everything in Q is nonetheless in the New Testament because it is in Matthew and Luke.

The reconstruction process tried to measure the degree of probability to be accorded to each of the thousands of decisions involved. As a result, rather complex marks in the text of the critical edition make clear just how probable each word was thought to be. Those wishing to study such technical details may consult that edition itself. But for average readers such intrusions into the flow of the text would distract more than inform, and so are reduced here to a strict minimum.

HOW TO USE THE SAYINGS GOSPEL Q

In what follows, references to the Sayings Gospel Q use the chapter and verse numeration of the Gospel of Luke, since it was Luke who usually followed the sequence of Q more faithfully than did Matthew. For example, the reference "Q 6:22" indicates that this is the Q version of the saying found in Luke 6:22 and its Matthean parallel Matthew 5:11.

In a few instances where the Matthean sequence diverges from that of Luke, it is Matthew who retains the sequence of Q. The result is that at times the sequence in which Q is reconstructed will have (Lukan) numeration that is not sequential, such as that for the three temptations of Jesus. In such cases, the verses are printed in Matthean sequence, since that is the sequence of Q, but the numeration still pedantically follows Luke, with the result that the sequence of the verse numeration is, for example, "Q 4:1–4, 9–12, 5–8, 13."

In one instance, a saying thought to belong to Q is nonetheless only in Matthew; it is listed between the immediately preceding and following Q sayings in Luke. "Q 6:29´30/Matthew 5:41" means that the Q saying behind Matthew 5:41 belongs in Q between 6:29 and 6:30, that is, between Luke 6:29 and 6:30.

If there is a high degree of uncertainty about a particular word or phrase, no text is provided, but the place is marked with an ellipsis,   , indicating that there was some text here. Parentheses, ( ), are used where the text has to be emended or where only the gist or train of thought, but not the actual language, could be provided.

To make it easier to find your way through the text, headings are inserted for each unit of associated sayings, clusters, or paragraphs. Of course they do not belong to the original text of the Sayings Gospel Q itself.

Beneath each section are given the chapter and verse references to Q. Since the chapter and verse reference to Q is the same as that of Luke, if you are interested in seeing the section in its Lukan context with its Lukan wording, you can simply look it up in that same chapter and verse in Luke. For example, the Lukan text making use of Q 6:20–21 is to be found in Luke 6:20–21.

References to Matthew are also added beneath each section. For example, "Q 6:20–21, see Matthew 5:1–4, 6" points to the verses in Matthew where these Q sayings are to be found. Thus, if you would like to see the way in which Matthew edited, and from his point of view improved, the wording of Q, you can see it for yourself. In this example, you can see how Matthew "spiritualized" the Beatitudes by shifting "the poor" and "hungry" to "poor in spirit" and "hungering and thirsting after righteousness." Or you can see how Matthew carries out the same kind of spiritualizing in the Lord's Prayer, "Q 11:2b–4, see Matthew 6:9–13a." In Matthew, Q's "let your reign come: Our day's bread give us today" becomes "let your reign come: your will be done on earth as it is in heaven; our day's bread give us today." Gradually, you will begin to get a feel for the emphases that Matthew does not want to be overlooked. Conversely, Luke has different emphases, which you can find if you compare the reading in Q with the reading in Luke.

Since a goodly number of the same sayings occur in the Sayings Gospel Q and in the *Gospel of Thomas,* the references to the *Gospel of Thomas* are added after the sections that have such parallels, just after the reference to Matthew, for example, "Q 6:20–21, see Matthew 5:1–4, 6, also *Thomas* 54; 69:2." In this case, *Thomas* saying 54 agrees with the Q Beatitude for the poor, but Saying 69:2 spells out in more detail the Beatitude for the hungry: "Blessed are those who hunger in order that the stomach of the one who craves for (food) may eat its fill."

To make the actual comparison with the reading in the *Gospel of Thomas,* let me refer you to *The Fifth Gospel: The Gospel of Thomas Comes of Age,* by Stephen J. Patterson and myself, with a new English translation by a team of scholars led by Hans-Gebhard Bethge, which we edited (Harrisburg, PA: Trinity Press International, 1998).

Later chapters contain a few quotations from the *Gospel of Thomas* (Nag Hammadi Codex II, Tractate 2) and the *Gospel of Philip* (Nag Hammadi Codex II, Tractate 3). Since holes in the papyrus occur, the missing or emended text is supplied in square brackets, [ ], when the reading is rather certain. When it is impossible to fill the hole with any certainty, the place is indicated with an ellipsis inside the square brackets, [. . .] .

THE TEXT OF THE SAYINGS GOSPEL Q

Opening Line

Opening Line

⁰ (. . . Jesus . . .)

Q 3:0, not in Matthew or Luke

The Introduction of John

²ᵇ (. . .) John ³ᵃ (. . .) all the region of the Jordan (. . .)

Q 3:2b–3a, see Matthew 3:1, 5

John's Announcement of Judgment

⁷ He said to the crowds coming to be baptized: Snakes' litter! Who warned you to run from the impending rage? ⁸ So bear fruit worthy of repentance, and do not presume to tell yourselves: We have as forefather Abraham! For I tell you: God can produce children for Abraham right out of these rocks! ⁹ And the ax already lies at the root of the trees. So every tree not bearing healthy fruit is to be chopped down and thrown on the fire.

Q 3:7–9, see Matthew 3:7–10

John and the One to Come

¹⁶ᵇ I baptize you in water, but the one to come after me is more powerful than I, whose sandals I am not fit to take off. He will

baptize you in holy Spirit and fire. [17] His pitchfork is in his hand, and he will clear his threshing floor and gather the wheat into his granary, but the chaff he will burn on a fire that can never be put out.

Q 3:16b–17, see Matthew 3:11–12

The Baptism of Jesus

[21b] Jesus . . . baptized, heaven opened, [22] and the Spirit . . . upon him . . . Son . . .

Q 3:21b–22, see Matthew 3:16–17

The Temptations of Jesus

[1] And Jesus was led into the wilderness by the Spirit [2] to be tempted by the devil. And he ate nothing for forty days; he became hungry. [3] And the devil told him: If you are God's Son, order that these stones become loaves. [4] And Jesus answered him: It is written: A person is not to live only from bread.

[9] The devil took him along to Jerusalem and put him on the tip of the temple and told him: If you are God's Son, throw yourself down. [10] For it is written: He will command his angels about you, [11] and on their hands they will bear you, so that you do not strike your foot against a stone. [12] And Jesus in reply told him: It is written: Do not put to the test the Lord your God.

[5] And the devil took him along to a very high mountain and showed him all the kingdoms of the world and their splendor, [6] and told him: All these I will give you, [7] if you bow down before me. [8] And in reply Jesus told him: It is written: Bow down to the Lord your God, and serve only him.

[13] And the devil left him.

Q 4:1–4, 9–12, 5–8, 13, see Matthew 4:1–11

Nazara

[16] (. . .) Nazara (. . .)

> Q 4:16, see Matthew 4:13

Beatitudes for the Poor, Hungry, and Mourning

[20] (. . .) And raising his eyes to his disciples he said· Blessed are you poor, for God's reign is for you. [21] Blessed are you who hunger, for you will eat your fill. Blessed are you who mourn, for you will be consoled.

> Q 6:20–21, see Matthew 5:1–4, 6, also
> *Thomas* 54; 69:2

The Beatitude for the Persecuted

[22] Blessed are you when they insult and persecute you, and say every kind of evil against you because of the son of humanity. [23] Be glad and exult, for vast is your reward in heaven. For this is how they persecuted the prophets who were before you.

> Q 6:22–23, see Matthew 5:11–12, also
> *Thomas* 69:1a; 68:1

Love Your Enemies

[27] Love your enemies [28] and pray for those persecuting you, [35c–d] so that you may become sons of your Father, for he raises his sun on bad and good and rains on the just and unjust.

> Q 6:27–28, 35c–d, see Matthew
> 5:44–45

Renouncing One's Own Rights

[29] The one who slaps you on the cheek, offer him the other as well; and to the person wanting to take you to court and get your shirt, turn over to him the coat as well. [29 ⁓ 30/Matt. 5:41] And the one who conscripts you for one mile, go with him a second. [30] To the one who asks of you, give; and from the one who borrows, do not ask back what is yours.

> Q 6:29, 29 ´ 30/Matthew 5:41, 30, see
> Matthew 5:39b–42, also *Thomas* 95

The Golden Rule

[31] And the way you want people to treat you, that is how you treat them.

> Q 6:31, see Matthew 7:12, also *Thomas* 6:3

Impartial Love

[32] If you love those loving you, what reward do you have? Do not even tax collectors do the same? [34] And if you lend to those from whom you hope to receive, what (reward do) you (have)? Do not even the Gentiles do the same?

> Q 6:32, 34, see Matthew 5:46, 47, also
> *Thomas* 95

Being Full of Pity Like Your Father

[36] Be full of pity, just as your Father is full of pity.

> Q 6:36, see Matthew 5:48

Not Judging

[37] Do not pass judgment, so you are not judged. For with what judgment you pass judgment, you will be judged. [38] And with the measurement you use to measure out, it will be measured out to you.

Q 6:37–38, see Matthew 7:1–2

The Blind Leading the Blind

[39] Can a blind person show the way to a blind person? Will not both fall into a pit?

Q 6:39, see Matthew 15:14, also *Thomas* 34

The Disciple and the Teacher

[40] A disciple is not superior to the teacher. It is enough for the disciple that he become like his teacher.

Q 6:40, see Matthew 10:24–25a

The Speck and the Beam

[41] And why do you see the speck in your brother's eye, but the beam in your own eye you overlook? [42] How can you say to your brother: Let me throw out the speck from your eye—and just look at the beam in your own eye? Hypocrite, first throw out from your own eye the beam, and then you will see clearly to throw out the speck in your brother's eye.

Q 6:41–42, see Matthew 7:3–5, also *Thomas* 26

The Tree Is Known by Its Fruit

[43] No healthy tree bears rotten fruit, nor on the other hand does a decayed tree bear healthy fruit. [44] For from the fruit the tree is known. Are figs picked from thorns, or grapes from thistles? [45] The good person from one's good treasure casts up good things, and the evil person from the evil treasure casts up evil things. For from exuberance of heart one's mouth speaks.

Q 6:43–45, see Matthew 7:16b, 18;
12:33b–35, also *Thomas* 45

Not Just Saying Master, Master

[46] Why do you call me: Master, Master, and do not do what I say?
Q 6:46, see Matthew 7:21

Houses Built on Rock or Sand

[47] Everyone hearing my sayings and acting on them [48] is like a person who built one's house on bedrock; and the rain poured down and the flash floods came, and the winds blew and pounded that house, and it did not collapse, for it was founded on bedrock. [49] And everyone who hears my sayings and does not act on them is like a person who built one's house on the sand; and the rain poured down and the flash floods came, and the winds blew and battered that house, and promptly it collapsed, and its fall was devastating.

Q 6:47–49, see Matthew 7:24–27

The Centurion's Faith in Jesus' Word

[1] And it came to pass when he ended these sayings, he entered Capernaum. [3] There came to him a centurion exhorting him and

saying: My boy (is) doing badly. And he said to him: Am I, by coming, to heal him? *⁶ᵇ⁻ᶜ* And in reply the centurion said: Master, I am not worthy for you to come under my roof; *⁷* but say the word, and let my boy be healed. *⁸* For I too am a person under authority, with soldiers under me, and I say to one: Go, and he goes, and to another: Come, and he comes, and to my slave: Do this, and he does it. *⁹* But Jesus, on hearing, was amazed, and said to those who followed: I tell you: Not even in Israel have I found such faith.

Q 7:1, 3, 6b–9, see Matthew 7:28a;
8:5–10

John's Inquiry About the One to Come

¹⁸ And John, on hearing about all these things, sending through his disciples, *¹⁹* said to him: Are you the one to come, or are we to expect someone else? *²²* And in reply he said to them: Go report to John what you hear and see: The blind regain their sight and the lame walk around, the skin-diseased are cleansed and the deaf hear, and the dead are raised, and the poor are evangelized. *²³* And blessed is whoever is not offended by me.

Q 7:18–19, 22–23, see Matthew 11:2–6

John—More Than a Prophet

²⁴ And when they had left, he began to talk to the crowds about John: What did you go out into the wilderness to look at? A reed shaken by the wind? *²⁵* If not, what *did* you go out to see? A person arrayed in finery? Look, those wearing finery are in kings' houses. *²⁶* But then what did you go out to see? A prophet? Yes, I tell you, even more than a prophet! *²⁷* This is the one about whom it has been written: Look, I am sending my messenger ahead of you, who will prepare your path in front of you. *²⁸* I tell you: There has not arisen among women's offspring anyone who surpasses John.

Yet the least significant in God's kingdom is more than he.

> Q 7:24–28, see Matthew 11:7–11, also
> Thomas 78; 46

For and Against John

²⁹ For John came to you, . . . the tax collectors and . . . (responded positively) ³⁰ but the (religious authorities rejected) him.

> Q 7:29–30, see Matthew 21:32

This Generation and the Children of Wisdom

³¹ To what am I to compare this generation and what is it like? ³² It is like children seated in the marketplaces, who, addressing the others, say: We fluted for you, but you would not dance; we wailed, but you would not cry. ³³ For John came, neither eating nor drinking, and you say: He has a demon! ³⁴ The son of humanity came, eating and drinking, and you say: Look! A person who is a glutton and drunkard, a chum of tax collectors and sinners! ³⁵ But Wisdom was vindicated by her children.

> Q 7:31–35, see Matthew 11:16–19

Confronting Potential Followers

⁵⁷ And someone said to him: I will follow you wherever you go. ⁵⁸ And Jesus said to him: Foxes have holes, and birds of the sky have nests; but the son of humanity does not have anywhere he can lay his head. ⁵⁹ But another said to him: Master, permit me first to go and bury my father. ⁶⁰ But he said to him: Follow me, and leave the dead to bury their own dead.

> Q 9:57–60, see Matthew 8:19–22, also
> Thomas 86

Workers for the Harvest

² He said to his disciples: The harvest is plentiful, but the workers are few. So ask the Lord of the harvest to dispatch workers into his harvest.

Q 10:2, see Matthew 9:37–38, also
Thomas 73

Sheep Among Wolves

³ Be on your way! Look, I send you like sheep in the midst of wolves.

Q 10:3, see Matthew 10:16

No Provisions

⁴ Carry no purse, nor knapsack, nor sandals, nor stick, and greet no one on the road.

Q 10:4, see Matthew 10:9–10a

What to Do in Houses and Towns

⁵ Into whatever house you enter, first say: Peace to this house! ⁶ And if a son of peace be there, let your peace come upon him; but if not, let your peace return upon you. ⁷ And at that house remain, eating and drinking whatever they provide, for the worker is worthy of one's reward. Do not move around from house to house. ⁸ And whatever town you enter and they take you in, eat what is set before you. ⁹ And cure the sick there, and say to them: God's reign has reached unto you.

Q 10:5–9, see Matthew 10:7–8,
10b–13, also *Thomas* 14:4

Response to a Town's Rejection

[10] But into whatever town you enter and they do not take you in, on going out from that town, [11] shake off the dust from your feet. [12] I tell you: For Sodom it shall be more bearable on that day than for that town.

Q 10:10–12, see Matthew 10:14–15

Woes Against Galilean Towns

[13] Woe to you, Chorazin! Woe to you, Bethsaida! For if the wonders performed in you had taken place in Tyre and Sidon, they would have repented long ago, in sackcloth and ashes. [14] Yet for Tyre and Sidon it shall be more bearable at the judgment than for you. [15] And you, Capernaum, up to heaven will you be exalted? Into Hades shall you come down!

Q 10:13–15, see Matthew 11:21–24

Whoever Takes You in Takes Me In

[16] Whoever takes you in takes me in, and whoever takes me in takes in the one who sent me.

Q 10:16, see Matthew 10:40

Thanksgiving That God Reveals Only to Children

[21] At (that time) he said: I praise you, Father, Lord of heaven and earth, for you hid these things from sages and the learned, and disclosed them to children. Yes, Father, for that is what it has pleased you to do.

Q 10:21, see Matthew 11:25–26

Knowing the Father Through the Son

²² Everything has been entrusted to me by my Father, and no one knows the Son except the Father, nor does anyone know the Father except the Son, and to whomever the Son chooses to reveal him.

Q 10:22, see Matthew 11:27, also
Thomas 61:3b

The Beatitude for the Eyes That See

²³ᵇ Blessed are the eyes that see what you see. ²⁴ For I tell you: Many prophets and kings wanted to see what you see, but never saw it, and to hear what you hear, but never heard it.

Q 10:23b–24, see Matthew 13:16–17

The Lord's Prayer

²ᵇ When you pray, say: Father—may your name be kept holy!—let your reign come: ³ Our day's bread give us today; ⁴ and cancel our debts for us, as we too have canceled for those in debt to us; and do not put us to the test!

Q 11:2b–4, see Matthew 6:9–13a

The Certainty of the Answer to Prayer

[9] I tell you: Ask and it will be given to you, search and you will find, knock and it will be opened to you. [10] For everyone who asks receives, and the one who searches finds, and to the one who knocks will it be opened. [11] What person of you, whose child asks for bread, will give him a stone? [12] Or again when he asks for a fish, will give him a snake? [13] So if you, though evil, know how to give good gifts to your children, by how much more will the Father from heaven give good things to those who ask him!

Q 11:9–13, see Matthew 7:7–11, also
Thomas 92:1; 94

Refuting the Beelzebul Accusation

[14] And he cast out a demon which made a person mute. And once the demon was cast out, the mute person spoke. And the crowds were amazed. [15] But some said: By Beelzebul, the ruler of demons, he casts out demons! [17] But, knowing their thoughts, he said to them: Every kingdom divided against itself is left barren, and every household divided against itself will not stand. [18] And if Satan is divided against himself, how will his kingdom stand? [19] And if I by Beelzebul cast out demons, your sons, by whom do they cast them out? This is why they will be your judges. [20] But if it is by the finger of God that I cast out demons, then there has come upon you God's reign.

Q 11:14–15, 17–20, see Matthew
9:32–34; 12:25–28

Looting a Strong Person's House

²¹ (A strong person's house cannot be looted, ²² but if someone still stronger overpowers him, he does get looted.)

> Q 11:21–22, see Matthew 12:29, also
> *Thomas* 35

The One Not with Me

²³ The one not with me is against me, and the one not gathering with me scatters.

> Q 11:23, see Matthew 12:30

The Return of the Unclean Spirit

²⁴ When the defiling spirit has left the person, it wanders through waterless regions looking for a resting place, and finds none. Then it says: I will return to my house from which I came. ²⁵ And on arrival it finds it swept and tidied up. ²⁶ Then it goes and brings with it seven other spirits more evil than itself, and, moving in, they settle there. And the last circumstances of that person become worse than the first.

> Q 11:24–26, see Matthew 12:43–45

Hearing and Keeping God's Word

²⁷⁻²⁸ . . .

> Q 11:27–28, not in Matthew, but see
> *Thomas* 79:1–2

The Sign of Jonah for This Generation

[16] But some were demanding from him a sign. [29] But he said: This generation is an evil generation; it demands a sign, but a sign will not be given to it—except the sign of Jonah! [30] For as Jonah became to the Ninevites a sign, so also will the son of humanity be to this generation.

Q 11:16, 29–30, see Matthew 12:38–40

Something More Than Solomon and Jonah

[31] The queen of the South will be raised at the judgment with this generation and condemn it, for she came from the ends of the earth to listen to the wisdom of Solomon, and look, something more than Solomon is here! [32] Ninevite men will arise at the judgment with this generation and condemn it, for they repented at the announcement of Jonah, and look, something more than Jonah is here!

Q 11:31–32, see Matthew 12:41–42

The Light on the Lamp Stand

[33] No one lights a lamp and puts it in a hidden place, but on the lamp stand, and it gives light for everyone in the house.

Q 11:33, see Matthew 5:15, also Thomas
33:2–3

The Jaundiced Eye Darkens the Body's Radiance

³⁴ The lamp of the body is the eye. If your eye is generous, your whole body is radiant; but if your eye is jaundiced, your whole body is dark. ³⁵ So if the light within you is dark, how great must the darkness be!

> Q 11:34–35, see Matthew 6:22–23, also
> *Thomas* 24.3

Woes Against the Pharisees

⁴² Woe to you, Pharisees, for you tithe mint and dill and cumin, and give up justice and mercy and faithfulness. But these one had to do, without giving up those. ³⁹ᵇ Woe to you, Pharisees, for you purify the outside of the cup and dish, but inside they are full of plunder and dissipation. ⁴¹ Purify the inside of the cup, . . . its outside . . . pure. ⁴³ Woe to you, Pharisees, for you love the place of honor at banquets and the front seat in the synagogues and accolades in the markets. ⁴⁴ Woe to you, Pharisees, for you are like indistinct tombs and people walking on top are unaware.

> Q 11:42, 39b, 41, 43–44, see Matthew
> 23:23, 25, 26b–27, 6–7, also *Thomas*
> 89:1

Woes Against the Exegetes of the Law

[46b] And woe to you, exegetes of the Law, for you bind . . . burdens, and load on the backs of people, but you yourselves do not want to lift your finger to move them. [52] Woe to you, exegetes of the Law, for you shut the kingdom of (God) from people; you did not go in, nor let in those trying to get in. [47] Woe to you, for you built the tombs of the prophets, but your forefathers killed them. [48] Thus you witness against yourselves that you are the sons of your forefathers.

> Q 11:46b, 52, 47–48, see Matthew 23:4,
> 13, 29–32, also *Thomas* 39:1–2

Wisdom's Judgment on This Generation

[49] Therefore also Wisdom said: I will send them prophets and sages, and some of them they will kill and persecute, [50] so that a settling of accounts for the blood of all the prophets poured out from the founding of the world may be required of this generation, [51] from the blood of Abel to the blood of Zechariah, murdered between the sacrificial altar and the House. Yes, I tell you: An accounting will be required of this generation!

> Q 11:49–51, see Matthew 23:34–36

Proclaiming What Was Whispered

[2] Nothing is covered up that will not be exposed, and hidden that will not be known. [3] What I say to you in the dark, speak in the light; and what you hear whispered in the ear, proclaim on the housetops.

> Q 12:2–3, see Matthew 10:26–27, also
> *Thomas* 5:2 = 6:5; 33:1

Not Fearing the Body's Death

⁴ And do not be afraid of those who kill the body, but cannot kill the soul. ⁵ But fear the one who is able to destroy both the soul and body in Gehenna.

Q 12:4–5, see Matthew 10:28

More Precious Than Many Sparrows

⁶ Are not five sparrows sold for two cents? And yet not one of them will fall to earth without your Father's consent. ⁷ But even the hairs of your head all are numbered. Do not be afraid, you are worth more than many sparrows.

Q 12:6–7, see Matthew 10:29–31

Confessing or Denying

⁸ Anyone who may speak out for me in public, the son of humanity will also speak out for him before the angels. ⁹ But whoever may deny me in public will be denied before the angels.

Q 12:8–9, see Matthew 10:32–33

Speaking Against the Holy Spirit

¹⁰ And whoever says a word against the son of humanity, it will be forgiven him; but whoever speaks against the holy Spirit, it will not be forgiven him.

Q 12:10, see Matthew 12:32a–b, also
Thomas 44

Hearings Before Synagogues

[11] When they bring you before synagogues, do not be anxious about how or what you are to say; [12] for the holy Spirit will teach you in that hour what you are to say.

Q 12:11–12, see Matthew 10:19

Storing Up Treasures in Heaven

[33] Do not treasure for yourselves treasures on earth, where moth and gnawing deface and where robbers dig through and rob, but treasure for yourselves treasures in heaven, where neither moth nor gnawing defaces and where robbers do not dig through nor rob. [34] For where your treasure is, there will also be your heart.

Q 12:33–34, see Matthew 6:19–21, also
Thomas 76:3

Free from Anxiety Like Ravens and Lilies

[22b] Therefore I tell you, do not be anxious about your life, what you are to eat, nor about your body, with what you are to clothe yourself. [23] Is not life more than food, and the body than clothing? [24] Consider the ravens: They neither sow nor reap nor gather into barns, and yet God feeds them. Are you not better than the birds? [25] And who of you by being anxious is able to add to one's stature a cubit? [26] And why are you anxious about clothing? [27] Observe the lilies, how they grow: They do not work nor do they spin. Yet I tell you: Not even Solomon in all his glory was arrayed like one of these. [28] But if in the field the grass, there today and tomorrow thrown into the oven, God clothes thus, will he not much more clothe you, persons of petty faith! [29] So do not be anxious, saying: What are we to eat? Or: What are we to drink? Or: What are we to wear? [30] For all these the Gentiles seek; for your

Father knows that you need them all. ³¹ But seek his kingdom, and all these shall be granted to you.

> Q 12:22b–31, see Matthew 6:25–33,
> also *Thomas* 36:1, 4, 2–3

The Son of Humanity Comes as a Robber

³⁹ But know this: If the householder had known in which watch the robber was coming, he would not have let his house be dug into. ⁴⁰ You also must be ready, for the son of humanity is coming at an hour you do not expect.

> Q 12:39–40, see Matthew 24:43–44,
> also *Thomas* 21:5; 103

The Faithful or Unfaithful Slave

⁴² Who then is the faithful and wise slave whom the master put over his household to give them food on time? ⁴³ Blessed is that slave whose master, on coming, will find him so doing. ⁴⁴ Amen, I tell you: He will appoint him over all his possessions. ⁴⁵ But if that slave says in his heart: My master is delayed, and begins to beat his fellow slaves, and eats and drinks with the drunkards, ⁴⁶ the master of that slave will come on a day he does not expect and at an hour he does not know, and will cut him to pieces and give him an inheritance with the faithless.

> Q 12:42–46, see Matthew 24:45–51

Children Against Parents

[49] Fire have I come to hurl on the earth, and how I wish it had already blazed up! [51] Do you think that I have come to hurl peace on earth? I did not come to hurl peace, but a sword! [53] For I have come to divide son against father, and daughter against her mother, and daughter-in-law against her mother-in-law.

> Q 12:49, 51, 53, see Matthew 10:34–35,
> also *Thomas* 10; 16:1–2, 3b

Judging the Time

[54] But he said to them: When evening has come, you say: Good weather! For the sky is flame red. [55] And at dawn: Today it's wintry! For the lowering sky is flame red. [56] The face of the sky you know to interpret, but the time you are not able to?

> Q 12:54–56, see Matthew 16:2–3, also
> *Thomas* 91:2

Settling out of Court

[58] While you go along with your opponent on the way, make an effort to get loose from him, lest the opponent hand you over to the judge, and the judge to the assistant, and the (assistant) throw you into prison. [59] I say to you: You will not get out of there until you pay the last penny!

> Q 12:58–59, see Matthew 5:25–26

The Mustard Seed

[18] What is the kingdom of God like, and with what am I to compare it? [19] It is like a seed of mustard, which a person took and threw into his garden. And it grew and developed into a tree, and the birds of the sky nested in its branches.

> Q 13:18–19, see Matthew 13:31–32, also *Thomas* 20

The Yeast

[20] And again: With what am I to compare the kingdom of God? [21] It is like yeast, which a woman took and hid in three measures of flour until it was fully fermented.

> Q 13:20–21, see Matthew 13:33, also *Thomas* 96:1–2

I Do Not Know You

[24] Enter through the narrow door, for many will seek to enter and few are those who (enter through) it. [25] When the householder has arisen and locked the door, and you begin to stand outside and knock on the door, saying: Master, open for us, and he will answer you: I do not know you, [26] then you will begin saying: We ate in your presence and drank, and it was in our streets you taught. [27] And he will say to you: I do not know you! Get away from me, you who do lawlessness!

> Q 13:24–27, see Matthew 7:13–14, 22–23; 25:10–12

Many Shall Come from Sunrise and Sunset

²⁹ And many shall come from Sunrise and Sunset and recline ²⁸ with Abraham and Isaac and Jacob in the kingdom of God, but you will be thrown out into the outer darkness, where there will be wailing and grinding of teeth.

Q 13:29, 28, see Matthew 8:11–12

The Reversal of the Last and the First

³⁰ The last will be first, and the first last.

Q 13:30, see Matthew 20:16, also
Thomas 4:2

Judgment over Jerusalem

³⁴ O Jerusalem, Jerusalem, who kills the prophets and stones those sent to her! How often I wanted to gather your children together, as a hen gathers her nestlings under her wings, and you were not willing! ³⁵ Look, your House is forsaken! I tell you: You will not see me until (the time) comes when you say: Blessed is the one who comes in the name of the Lord!

Q 13:34–35, see Matthew 23:37–39

The Exalted Humbled and the Humble Exalted

¹¹ Everyone exalting oneself will be humbled, and the one humbling oneself will be exalted.

Q 14:11, see Matthew 23:12

The Invited Dinner Guests

¹⁶ A certain person prepared a large dinner, and invited many. ¹⁷ And he sent his slave at the time of the dinner to say to the invited: Come, for it is now ready. ¹⁸ (One declined because of his) farm. ¹⁹ (Another declined because of his business.) ²¹ And the slave, (on coming, said) these things to his master. Then the householder, enraged, said to his slave: ²³ Go out on the roads, and whomever you find, invite, so that my house may be filled.

> *Q 14:16–18, 19, 21, 23*, see Matthew
> 22:2–3, 5, 7a, 8–10, also *Thomas* 64

Hating One's Family

²⁶ (The one who) does not hate father and mother (can)not (be) my (disciple); and (the one who does not hate) son and daughter cannot be my disciple.

> *Q 14:26*, see Matthew 10:37, also
> *Thomas* 55; 101:1–2

Taking One's Cross

²⁷ The one who does not take one's cross and follow after me cannot be my disciple.

> *Q 14:27*, see Matthew 10:38, also
> *Thomas* 55:2

Finding or Losing One's Life

³³ The one who finds one's life will lose it, and the one who loses one's life for my sake will find it.

> *Q 17:33*, see Matthew 10:39

Insipid Salt

[34] Salt is good; but if salt becomes insipid, with what will it be seasoned? [35] Neither for the earth nor for the dunghill is it fit—it gets thrown out.

Q 14:34–35, see Matthew 5:13

God or Mammon

[13] Nobody can serve two masters; for a person will either hate the one and love the other, or be devoted to the one and despise the other. You cannot serve God and Mammon.

Q 16:13, see Matthew 6:24, also *Thomas* 47:2

Since John the Kingdom of God

[16] The Law and the Prophets were until John. From then on the kingdom of God is violated and the violent plunder it.

Q 16:16, see Matthew 11:12–13

No Serif of the Law to Fall

[17] But it is easier for heaven and earth to pass away than for one iota or one serif of the Law to fall.

Q 16:17, see Matthew 5:18

Divorce Leading to Adultery

[18] Everyone who divorces his wife and marries another commits adultery, and the one who marries a divorcée commits adultery.

Q 16:18, see Matthew 5:32

Against Enticing Little Ones

[1] It is necessary for enticements to come, but woe to the one through whom they come! [2] It is better for him if a millstone is put around his neck and he is thrown into the sea, than that he should entice one of these little ones.

Q 17:1–2, see Matthew 18:7, 6

The Lost Sheep

[4] Which person is there among you who has a hundred sheep, on losing one of them, will not leave the ninety-nine in the mountains and go hunt for the lost one? [5a] And if it should happen that he finds it, [7] I say to you that he rejoices over it more than over the ninety-nine that did not go astray.

Q 15:4–5a, 7, see Matthew 18:12–13,
also Thomas 107

The Lost Coin

[8] Or what woman who has ten coins, if she were to lose one coin, would not light a lamp and sweep the house and hunt until she finds? [9] And on finding she calls the friends and neighbors, saying: Rejoice with me, for I found the coin which I had lost. [10] Just so, I tell you, there is joy before the angels over one repenting sinner.

Q 15:8–10, not in Matthew

Forgiving a Sinning Brother Repeatedly

[3] If your brother sins against you, rebuke him; and if he repents, forgive him. [4] And if seven times a day he sins against you, also seven times shall you forgive him.

Q 17:3–4, see Matthew 18:15, 21

Faith Like a Mustard Seed

[6] If you have faith like a mustard seed, you might say to this mulberry tree: Be uprooted and planted in the sea! And it would obey you.

> Q 17:6, see Matthew 17:20b, also
> *Thomas* 48

The Kingdom of God Within You

[20] But on being asked when the kingdom of God is coming, he answered them and said: The kingdom of God is not coming visibly. [21] Nor will one say: Look, here! Or: There! For, look, the kingdom of God is within you!

> Q 17:20–21, see Matthew 24:23, also
> *Thomas* 3:1–3; 113

The Son of Humanity Like Lightning

[23] If they say to you: Look, he is in the wilderness, do not go out; look, he is indoors, do not follow. [24] For as the lightning streaks out from Sunrise and flashes as far as Sunset, so will the son of humanity be on his day.

> Q 17:23–24, see Matthew 24:26–27,
> also *Thomas* 3:1–2

Vultures Around a Corpse

[37] Wherever the corpse, there the vultures will gather.

> Q 17:37, see Matthew 24:28

As in the Days of Noah

²⁶ As it took place in the days of Noah, so will it be in the day of the son of humanity. ²⁷ For as in those days they were eating and drinking, marrying and giving in marriage, until the day Noah entered the ark and the flood came and took them all, ³⁰ so will it also be on the day the son of humanity is revealed.

Q 17.26 27, 30, see Matthew 24.37–39

One Taken, One Left

³⁴ I tell you: There will be two men in the field; one is taken and one is left. ³⁵ Two women will be grinding at the mill; one is taken and one is left.

Q 17:34–35, see Matthew 24:40–41,
also *Thomas* 61:1

The Entrusted Money

¹² A certain person, on taking a trip, ¹³ called ten of his slaves and gave them ten minas and said to them: Do business until I come. ¹⁵ After a long time the master of those slaves comes and settles accounts with them. ¹⁶ And the first came saying: Master, your mina has produced ten more minas. ¹⁷ And he said to him: Well done, good slave, you have been faithful over a little, I will set you over much. ¹⁸ And the second came saying: Master, your mina has earned five minas. ¹⁹ He said to him: Well done, good slave, you have been faithful over a little, I will set you over much. ²⁰ And the other came saying: Master, ²¹ I knew you, that you are a hard person, reaping where you did not sow and gathering up from where you did not winnow; and, scared, I went and hid your (mina) in the ground. Here, you have what belongs to you. ²² He said to him: Wicked slave! You knew that I reap where I have not sown, and

gather up from where I have not winnowed? [23] Then you had to invest my money with the money changers! And at my coming I would have received what belongs to me plus interest. [24] So take from him the mina and give it to the one who has the ten minas. [26] For to everyone who has will be given; but from the one who does not have, even what he has will be taken from him.

> Q 19:12–13, 15–24, 26, see Matthew
> 25:14–15b, 19–29, also *Thomas* 41

You Will Judge the Twelve Tribes of Israel

[28] You who have followed me [30] will sit on thrones judging the twelve tribes of Israel.

> Q 22:28, 30, see Matthew 19:28

THREE

JESUS WAS A GALILEAN JEW

We of course all realize that Jesus was a Jew. But, since the New Testament is a gentile Christian book, we probably do not realize just how pervasive his Jewish lifestyle was in actual practice, for after a few generations the bulk of Christians were Gentiles. Indeed, they succeeded in weeding out as heretics Jewish Christians who continued Jewish practices such as circumcision and Sabbath observance, even though Jesus himself had observed such practices. So it may not be out of place to list Jesus' Jewish traits that the gentile Gospels nonetheless do report.

The best way to be a Jew is to have a Jewish mother. Jesus' mother's name in Greek is Maria, sometimes Mariam, which is the Greek spelling of Miriam, the name of Moses' sister. She came from an Aramaic-speaking Jewish hamlet in Galilee called Nazara.

JESUS' MOTHER TONGUE, ARAMAIC

Jesus' mother tongue was Aramaic, for Hebrew was no longer spoken colloquially by the Jewish population at that time. In that part of the world it was Aramaic, a kindred Semitic language, that had become the everyday language shared by the various populations. It varied slightly from region to region, much as does Arabic today in that area. As a result, Peter at the trial could be recognized as a Galilean by the sound of his voice.[1] But practically no Galilean Aramaic of the first century has survived in writing, no doubt in large part because the native population was for all practical purposes illiterate.

Some of the characters in the story still have their Aramaic names, for it was a custom then, as now, to name people after their father or male ancestor. This is called a patronymic. Patronymics are prevalent in modern Arabic, in which a person's "second" name is really his father's "first" name. And patronymics are still prevalent in European languages. My full name has two such patronymics: James *McConkey Robinson.* Patronymics tend to survive even in foreign languages although everything else is translated. The Gaelic *Mac* or *Mc,* meaning "son," survives in Scottish and Irish, and even in American English!

The Aramaic word for "son" was *bar,* and so all the personal names beginning with *Bar-* simply name a person after that person's father. The Greek word for foreigner was "barbarian," which may well reflect the prevalence of Aramaic in the eastern Mediterranean, where so many names began with *Bar-.* Greeks could well say to themselves, "*Bar-*this and *Bar-*that, they are all *bar-bar-*ians to me!"

A survey of these names in the New Testament gives perhaps the clearest impression of the prevalence of Aramaic in Jesus' world, since the New Testament itself was written in Greek. Simon Peter is called Simon *Bar-*Jonah,[2] translated in the Gospel of John as "Simon son of John"[3] or simply "John's Simon."[4] *Barti-maeus*'s name is given in Aramaic and translated "son of Timaeus."[5] When Barnabas is first introduced, his full name is given: "Joseph, surnamed by the apostles *Barnabas* (which means 'Son of Encouragement')."[6] "*Bar-Jesus*" is given as the Aramaic name of the sorcerer Elymas.[7] Other instances in which the patronymic is given in addition to someone's "own" name are "Joseph called *Barsabbas*, who is called Justus"[8] and "Judas called *Barsabbas*."[9] There are also persons whose only name is the patronymic: *Barabbas*[10] and *Bartholomew*.[11] Two in the list of the Twelve have the patronymic but only in Greek translation: "James the son of Alphaeus"[12] and "Judas the son of James."[13] In one instance, the patronymic is only in Greek, but then a Hebrew nickname is appended: "James son of Zebedee and John the brother of James (to whom he gave the name Boanerges, that is, Sons of Thunder)."[14] The Aramaic patronymic still flourishes today in the Jewish ritual celebrating adulthood, *bar* mitzvah, meaning "son of the commandment."

In addition to such patronymics, the Gospel of Mark preserves a few Aramaic terms Jesus used, no doubt because the original sound seemed more effective than a banal Greek translation. But the Greek translation is at times appended, and Matthew and Luke usually omit the Aramaic altogether in editing Mark for their Gospels. In Mark, when Jesus heals a deaf mute, the key Aramaic word he uses is retained, then translated into Greek:

> He took him aside in private, away from the crowd, and put his fingers into his ears, and he spat and touched his tongue. Then looking up to heaven, he sighed and said to him, "*Eph-phatha*," that is, "Be opened."[15]

Matthew reports at this place only that sick people were brought to Jesus:

> . . . and he cured them.[16]

Luke omits the story completely. In Mark, the healing of Jairus's daughter is effected with an Aramaic expression, which is translated into Greek:

> He took her by the hand and said to her, "*Talitha cum,*" which means, "Little girl, get up!"[17]

The Gospel of Luke edits out the Aramaic:

> But he took her up by the hand and called out, "Child, get up!"[18]

But then in Acts Luke uses a variant spelling of the Aramaic term as the "native" name of a woman named (in Greek) Dorcas, whom Peter raises from the dead apparently by using the same potent Aramaic expression Jesus had used:

> Now in Joppa there was a disciple whose name was *Tabitha,* which in Greek is Dorcas. . . . Peter put all of them outside, and then he knelt down and prayed. He turned to the body and said, "*Tabitha,* get up." Then she opened her eyes, and seeing Peter, she sat up.[19]

Talitha or *Tabitha* may well have become no more than a powerful-sounding term still used, due to its potency, in Christian healings, even when they took place in Greek. This may seem strange to us, but it would not have been unusual in antiquity. Greek magic papyri have formulas loaded with such foreign ("barbaric") terms, whose very sound was counted on to perform curses, cures, or other superhuman transactions, although the literal meaning was no longer understood.

In the garden of Gethsemane, Jesus' prayer addresses God in Aramaic, according to Mark:

And he said, "*Abba,* Father, for you all things are possible; remove this cup from me; yet, not what I want, but what you want."[20]

Matthew and Luke omit the Aramaic form of address:

And going a little farther, he threw himself on the ground and prayed, "My Father, if it is possible, let this cup pass from me; yet not what I want but what you want."

Then he withdrew from them about a stone's throw, knelt down, and prayed, "Father, if you are willing, remove this cup from me; yet, not my will but yours be done."[21]

Apparently Mark preferred to retain Aramaic formulas, but Matthew and Luke tended to omit them.

It must certainly be just a Greek translation of the familiar Hebrew/Aramaic greeting *Shalom* when the New Testament presents Jesus greeting people with "Peace" on knocking at a door to ask for bed and breakfast[22] and in appearances of the resurrection Christ;[23] it is still today used as a greeting by Jews (and indeed by many others as well).

The similarity of the language of Jesus' prayer in Gethsemane to the Lord's Prayer suggests that it too began *Abba.* But since the Lord's Prayer is not in Mark, but only in Matthew and Luke,[24] the Aramaic form of address to God is absent. Yet Paul on his own recalls the Aramaic term for addressing God, which does support the view that it continued to be used in early Christian prayer as the appropriate form of address:

When we cry, "*Abba!* Father!" it is the Spirit himself bearing witness with our spirit that we are children of God.[25]

Paul seems to realize that this is a usage going back to Jesus himself:

> And because you are children, God has sent the Spirit of his
> Son into our hearts, crying, "*Abba,* Father!"[26]

Paul also reports another Aramaic term probably still in use in the Greek liturgy of the early church, *Marana tha,* meaning "Lord, come!":

> Let anyone be accursed who has no love for the Lord.
> *Marana tha.*[27]

This occurs in Greek translation at the conclusion of the book of Revelation:

> The one who testifies to these things says, "Surely I am
> coming soon." Amen. Come, Lord Jesus![28]

This and other Aramaic expressions are preserved in the eucharistic prayers of an early Christian manual of church order (see Chapter 10):

> May grace come, and may this world pass away.
> *Hosanna* to the God of David.
> If anyone is holy, let him come;
> If anyone is not, let him repent.
> *Marana tha! Amen.*[29]

Hosanna is a Hebrew term of address to God meaning "Oh save!" But it had come to serve simply as an acclamation of Palm Sunday[30] based on a psalm of the Hebrew scriptures[31] (again, Luke omits the foreign term[32]). *Amen* is a Hebrew term meaning "Truly," sometimes translated into Greek in the New Testament, but more often left in Hebrew, as is our custom still today. Foreign-language terms do achieve a certain status as loanwords whose "feel" and potency would be lost in translation. In English we all would prefer to end a prayer with *Amen* rather than with "Truly."

Another such Hebrew exclamation is *Hallelujah,* meaning "Praise God."[33] Who wants to translate *Hosanna* and *Hallelujah?* So it is not surprising that the Gospels retain some Aramaic expressions documenting Jesus' mother tongue. The most poignant instance of Jesus' Aramaic to have survived is his cry of abandonment from the cross:

> And at three o'clock Jesus cried out with a loud voice, "*Eloi, Eloi, lema sabachthani?*" which means, "O my God, o my God, why have you abandoned me?"[34]

Jesus was addressed in the Gospels with the Hebrew or Aramaic *Rabbi* and twice with the more familiar *Rabbouni,* once in Mark[35] and once in John.[36] This was not yet a title for a Jewish "pastor" of a local synagogue, as in today's usage, but was simply a form of address that showed respect. The Gospel of John translates *Rabbi*[37] when it first occurs, and also *Rabbouni,*[38] in both cases: "which means Teacher."

There seems to be a clear aversion to *Rabbi* and *Rabbouni* on the part of Matthew and Luke. Once when Mark uses *Rabbouni* of Jesus,[39] both Matthew and Luke read "Lord."[40] Another time when Mark presents Peter addressing Jesus in the transfiguration story as *Rabbi,*[41] Matthew and Luke read "Lord."[42] In still another Markan instance of Peter addressing Jesus as *Rabbi,*[43] Matthew omits the address[44] and Luke omits the whole incident.

Only when Mark presents Judas addressing Jesus as *Rabbi*[45] does Matthew retain *Rabbi,*[46] but Luke omits here the address completely.[47] In fact, Luke never uses *Rabbi* anywhere. Matthew

actually inserts a second instance of Judas addressing Jesus as
Rabbi[48] where there is no parallel at all in the other Gospels. But
this is obviously because Judas has been disowned. This form of
address on the part of Judas merely documents his status as an
unworthy disciple.

Actually, Matthew explicitly rejects the use of *Rabbi* by arguing
that teachers of the Law and Pharisees seek to be so addressed
out of pride.[49] It is hence to be avoided:

> But you are not to be called *Rabbi,* for you have one teacher,
> and you are all brethren.[50]

This total avoidance by Luke and partial avoidance by Matthew
suggest that if *Rabbi* occurred in the Sayings Gospel Q, it may not
have survived for us to see, in that both Matthew and Luke may
well have altered or omitted it. This possibility suggests itself
most strongly in the one saying that focuses on the form of address:

> Why do you call me: "Master, Master," and do not do what I
> say?[51]

This may very well have read in the Sayings Gospel Q:

> Why do you call me: "*Rabbi, Rabbi,*" but do not do what I say?

But since such a wording is attested in neither Matthew nor
Luke, it cannot be ascribed to Q. It has to remain a tantalizing
speculation.

Modern translations carry even further this trend found in
Matthew and Luke to avoid addressing Jesus as *Rabbi* or *Rabbouni*.
In both Matthew and Mark (not to speak of Luke), the King
James translation and the Revised Standard Version never use

Rabbi in addressing Jesus, though in each case the New Revised Standard Version and the New English Bible have restored *Rabbi*.[52]

Rabbi is a more common form of address for Jesus in the Gospel of John.[53] And the Gospel of John once uses *Rabbi* to address John the Baptist.[54] In the case of the Gospel of John, modern translations have consistently translated *Rabbi,* though the King James translation fluctuates.

This use or avoidance of *Rabbi* illustrates the extent to which the Jewish world in which Jesus lived is visible though obscured in the Gospels then and now.

Jesus may have known some Greek, since it was becoming the cosmopolitan language of the eastern part of the Roman Empire, but it would not have been the language he normally used. In fact, the Galilean towns he went to with his message were the hamlets of the indigenous Aramaic-speaking population, not cosmopolitan cities where Greek would also have been readily spoken. The Gospels never mention such hellenized cities of Galilee as Sepphoris near Nazareth, Tiberias on the Sea of Galilee, or Scythopolis near the Jordan. Jesus may have avoided them.

JESUS' (IL)LITERACY

It is estimated that in the Roman Empire 10 to 15 percent of the population was literate (which normally meant Latin or Greek). Hence it is not very probable that the son of a carpenter in an Aramaic-speaking village in Galilee would have learned to read and write.

Nazareth has been calculated to have been a small hamlet of, at most, a couple hundred inhabitants. (Modern translations tend to call it a "town," obscuring the fact that the Evangelists use the Greek word for "city,"[55] since it was so important to them—Luke even has Paul score the point with King Agrippa that "this was not done in a corner."[56]) Hence it is not even clear whether Nazareth had a synagogue with a school in which Jesus could have learned enough Hebrew to read the Jewish scriptures.

In any case, Jesus was immersed in Jewish culture, for he would have soaked up the oral traditions of his village. Since we are flooded with written material, not to speak of video images, it is difficult for us to imagine the extent to which oral material lived on in an illiterate premodern population.

Perhaps an illustration will help. When we say someone has the "Midas touch" we mean someone for whom every business venture makes an enormous profit—without ever having read anything about the enormously wealthy Phrygian king whose legendary touch is said to have turned everything he touched into gold. We know this only from oral tradition, in this case thanks to its being preserved as a metaphor. Similarly, the expression "Not even Solomon in all his glory was arrayed like one of these"[57] would not have required one to have read about Solomon in the Hebrew scriptures[58]—for King Solomon lived on in Judaism, renowned for his legendary splendor.

But when scholars argue that sayings of Jesus allude to obscure passages in the Hebrew scriptures, this shows no more than their own erudition (or at least that they own a concordance, which Jesus did not)—while displaying their inability to imagine village life in Galilee.

There is one reference to Jesus writing, in the familiar story of the woman taken in adultery:

Jesus bent down and wrote with his finger on the ground.[59]

It is not even clear if this is intended as writing some message or just as scratching in the ground, for there is no reference to anyone reading what he wrote. This was just Jesus' way of refusing to accuse the woman and waiting to see if anyone would presume to be without sin and hence justified in casting the first stone. But the basic problem with this story is that it was not part of the original New Testament. It is not in the oldest and best manuscripts, but was added, at various places, by later scribes.[60] However, since it ended up in the medieval manuscripts used by the King James translators,[61] we are familiar with it, in a way that we are not familiar with most late additions to and alterations of the original text (namely, those absent from the manuscripts used by King James's translators). Most modern translations either leave it out or indicate in some way that it is not part of the original text. (The New Revised Standard Version uses double square brackets and a footnote saying, "The most ancient authorities lack 7:53–8:11.") Hence this story, first documented in later centuries, cannot be relied upon for evidence of Jesus' literacy.

On the other hand, when one turns to the oldest layer of sayings ascribed to Jesus in the Sayings Gospel Q, instead of scribal learnedness one finds a villager's intuitive insight into nature. The striking thing about Jesus' acumen is that it is based more on his observation of nature than on the Hebrew scriptures.

He learned about God everywhere, for he saw it all: sunshine and rain showers sent to the bad as well as the good;[62] the contrast between a speck and a beam;[63] a tree known by its fruit (figs from thorns? grapes from thistles?);[64] houses built on bedrock or sand;[65] a reed shaken by the wind;[66] sheep among wolves;[67] the dust on one's feet;[68] the lamp on a lamp stand;[69] the killing of sparrows worth only a dime a dozen;[70] the hairs on your head,[71] ravens and lilies that do nothing, trusting in God to care for them;[72] God clothing so beautifully the grass of the field, there today and tomorrow thrown into the oven;[73] the flame red evening sky pointing to good weather, but a flame red morning sky pointing to wintry weather;[74] the tiny mustard seed or pinch of yeast growing all out of proportion to the insignificant beginning;[75] salt becoming insipid;[76] the lost sheep (with ninety-nine left unattended in the mountains);[77] the flash of lightning;[78] and vultures circling around a corpse.[79] Clearly, the sayings of Jesus radiate with the devout and acute observation of a village peasant, not with a scholar's learnedness in the Hebrew scriptures. In fact, Jesus himself made the same distinction:

> I praise you, Father, Lord of heaven and earth, for you hid these things from sages and the learned, and disclosed them to children.[80]

The Evangelists wrote more than half a century after Jesus' public ministry, by which time the original disciples, made up largely of peasants and fishermen, had been replaced by second-generation Christians, some of whom at least were educated enough to write the Gospels in Greek. They would unconsciously have conceived of Jesus more like themselves than was actually the case—the first in a long line of those who imagine Jesus in their own image. The result was a Jesus learned in the scriptures.

Already Mark, writing for a gentile Christian audience, presents one instance of Jesus citing scripture in a debate with Pharisees:

> One sabbath he was going through the grain fields; and as they made their way his disciples began to pluck heads of grain. The Pharisees said to him, "Look, why are they doing what is not lawful on the sabbath?" And he said to them, "Have you never read what David did when he and his companions were hungry and in need of food? He entered the house of God, when Abiathar was high priest, and ate the bread of the Presence, which it is not lawful for any but the priests to eat, and he gave some to his companions." Then he said to them, "The sabbath was made for humanity, and not humanity for the sabbath; so the son of humanity is lord even of the sabbath.[81]

On the issue of divorce, Mark presents Jesus calling upon the
Pharisees to report on what they read in scripture. Pharisees were
of course part of the elite, who might well have been literate.
They cite the scriptural permission of divorce,[82] which Jesus then
rejects on the grounds that in the creation narratives husband
and wife are to be joined as one flesh.[83] But when the disciples
have Jesus alone, they ask for an explanation. Jesus clarifies,[84]
using a saying also found in the Sayings Gospel Q:

> Everyone who divorces his wife and marries another com-
> mits adultery, and the one who marries a divorcée commits
> adultery.[85]

No doubt this saying goes back to Jesus himself and is the point
of departure for this tradition, which then grows into a more
rabbinic-like debate in which scripture is cited against scripture.

The parable of the vineyard is told in Mark as an allegory of
the history of God's dealings with his people from a Christian
point of view. The tenants (the Jews) are replaced by others
(Christians) as custodians of (God's) vineyard as punishment for
killing the vineyard owner's son.[86] An added scriptural text functioned in the early church as a proof-text for Jesus' resurrection:

> The stone that the builders rejected has become the corner-
> stone; this was the Lord's doing, and it is amazing in our
> eyes.[87]

This allegorization is so extensive throughout the parable that
scholars despaired of ever being able to move behind the church's
allegory to reconstruct Jesus' parable out of which it had developed. But then the *Gospel of Thomas* did produce that preallegorical
parable! It may well go back to Jesus, but lacks the scriptural allu-
sions that color the allegory:

He said: "A [usurer] owned a vineyard. He gave it to some farmers so that they would work it (and) he might receive its fruit from them. He sent his servant so that the farmers might give him the fruit of the vineyard. They seized his servant, beat him, (and) almost killed him. The servant went (back and) told his master. His master said: 'Perhaps [they] did not recognize [him].' He sent another servant, (and) the farmers beat that other one as well. Then the master sent his son (and) said: 'Perhaps they will show respect for my son.' (But) those farmers, since they knew that he was the heir of the vineyard, seized him (and) killed him. Whoever has ears should hear."[88]

The proof-text for the resurrection follows as a separate saying. Clearly this is one instance in which the *Gospel of Thomas* presents a version closer to what Jesus actually said, in a form that lacks the scriptural learnedness presented by Mark.

Luke carried this scriptural learnedness considerably further. His ability to compose the psalms of his infancy narrative[89] in such clear dependence on the psalms of the Greek translation of the Old Testament makes it clear that, though he is the most gentile of the Evangelists, he had been steeped in the Jewish scriptures. If not an early convert to Judaism, he must at least have been a "God-fearer," a quite literate Gentile who had worshiped in the Jewish synagogue from childhood on.

According to Luke, the twelve-year-old Jesus is taken by his parents to Jerusalem at Passover, where he interrogated the teachers in the temple with such acumen that they were amazed at his understanding and answers.[90] Luke may very well have intended this to refer to Jesus' ability to cite scripture, as the passage is often interpreted, though this is not actually said. There are striking insights in the peasant sayings of Jesus listed above that could indeed have confounded scholarly exegetes of the Law.

In a debate between Jesus and a Jewish authority on the Law about how to gain eternal life, Jesus quotes the Jewish equivalent of a creed that Jews knew by heart.[91] But then to cinch the point, Luke does not have Jesus proceed in rabbinic fashion to quote supporting texts. Instead, Jesus told the parable of the good Samaritan.[92] And in fact this won over the authority on Jewish Law,[93] even though the Hebrew scripture in question could well have been argued to limit "neighbor" to those in one's own clan or tribe,[94] which would have excluded a Samaritan, whom Jesus nonetheless used as his role model of neighborliness—after all, one should love one's enemy![95]

Luke, alone among the Evangelists, presents Jesus beginning his public ministry with a sermon in the synagogue he assumes to be in Jesus' hometown.[96] After reading from the scriptures,[97] he closed the book, returned it to the attendant, sat down, and preached that he was the fulfillment of the prophecy he had read—a very good Christian sermon. This is precisely what Luke would have done in Jesus' name—and very likely did on any and every occasion, to judge by the sermons he composed in the book of Acts to put on the tongues of Peter and Paul.

Matthew brings this same kind of scriptural erudition to expression again and again, such as quoting and correcting scripture in the six "antitheses" of the Sermon on the Mount: "You have heard that it was said . . . , but I say to you . . ."[98] But the very fact that three of the six antitheses originally existed as sayings on their own,[99] without the antithetic formula referring to the Old Testament, indicates that the formula has been secondarily added.

Much the same paradox found in the Sayings Gospel Q[100] and in Luke[101] is also presented by John—an unlettered Jesus being so learned:

About the middle of the festival Jesus went up into the temple and began to teach. The Jews were astonished at it, saying, "How does this man have such learning, when he has never been taught?" Then Jesus answered them, "My teaching is not mine but his who sent me."[102]

A more literal translation for "have such learning" is "know his letters." The Evangelists clearly sensed the problem that Jesus was uneducated and yet had the true (Christian) understanding of scripture.

After the fall of Jerusalem, the debate between church and synagogue was well under way, and the educated Evangelists could not imagine that Jesus had not been just as erudite, indeed surely more so, than were they. So they presented his sayings in a form that they were sure would have been the way he wanted them presented. But the simpler form in which they occur in the Sayings Gospel Q is nearer to the way he actually presented them.

THE DEAD SEA SCROLLS

Actually, up until the discovery of the Dead Sea Scrolls in caves near the Dead Sea over half a century ago (between 1947 and 1956), there were hardly any Jewish texts from the time of Jesus with which his sayings could be compared, to put them in their Jewish context and show what they would have meant to Jewish ears. Almost nothing has survived of the Galilean Aramaic of Jesus' time except for the few expressions of Jesus listed above, since the Aramaic-speaking population was largely illiterate. Hebrew was no longer a colloquial language spoken on the streets, but rather a learned language used at the synagogue, perhaps comparable to church Latin.

In the Palestinian synagogue, the text from the Torah was read out in Hebrew, then translated into Aramaic so that the audience could understand it. But outside of Palestine, the translation would have been into Greek. The main first-century Jewish authors outside of Palestine had assimilated into Greco-Roman culture to the extent that they wrote in Greek rather than in Aramaic or Hebrew.

The two best-known authors of the first century are Philo and Josephus, both of whom wrote very extensively in Greek. Their writings have survived, preserved for posterity largely by Christians, for neither was very popular with the rabbis who preserved Jewish culture down through the centuries. Philo interpreted Moses as if he were a Platonist, since Philo himself was a Platonic philosopher living in Alexandria, Egypt. Josephus was the Jewish general who lost the war with Rome, surrendered rather than dying with his boots on, and as a prisoner of war was taken to Rome by the Romans. There he became turncoat, announcing that the Roman emperor was the Messiah, and then wrote, in Greek, books both on Jewish history and on the history of the war with Rome, in each case slanted toward readers in the Roman Empire more than to his fellow Jews.

We normally assume that aspects of Judaism presupposed in the New Testament can be clarified by reference to the Judaism of the day, which is of course valid so far as it goes. But in practice it actually does not go very far, due to the lack of Jewish texts of the time. Sometimes the New Testament text itself is the main documentation for the Judaism of the day. For example, the Gospels present Jesus going again and again into the synagogues of Galilee to deliver his message and heal the sick there. What do we know of Galilean first-century synagogues? Nothing! Not even archaeological ruins from that period have been uncovered. So all we know of first-century synagogues in Galilee is what we can learn from—the New Testament!

All of this changed dramatically with the discovery of the Dead Sea Scrolls. Most were written in Hebrew [!] by learned scholars, members of a sect of Jewish enthusiasts who expected the end of the world to come very soon. So they had withdrawn from the worldly city life of Jerusalem and its corrupt temple worship to wait in the purity of the desert for God to act. There, at the Wadi Qumran, they built their monastery, expecting God soon to lead them in battle so as to triumph over all such evil. (Instead, a Roman legion destroyed their monastery in 68 C.E.— today the ruins are a tourist attraction.)

Thanks to the Dead Sea Scrolls, we now have an overwhelming mass of Jewish texts of the first two centuries before the Christian era and the first century of the Christian era, down to the destruction of the monastery. In caves near the monastery itself, these very highly educated Jewish monks spent their lives copying out the Hebrew scriptures, writing commentaries on them, and writing about their own group as the fulfillment of scriptural prophecy. Copies of almost all of the Hebrew scriptures have turned up in the jars found in the caves, and these copies are about a thousand years older than the oldest Hebrew copies known before! This alone would make of the Dead Sea Scrolls a tremendous sensation. But the scrolls also reveal that in such learned circles Hebrew was still being used for their own writings, which would hardly have been expected by modern scholars.

All this learnedness is very different from what is found among Jesus and his immediate followers, who not only were not learned scholars, but were largely illiterate—they could not have read the scrolls if they had seen them! But, conversely, these learned monks were completely engrossed in their work and hardly saw the world around them. From their hillside overlooking the Dead Sea, they gazed out at this dramatic scene every day, but never mention the fact or describe the landscape. You would never know by reading the scrolls that they were written in a wadi overlooking the Dead Sea. If they had not been discovered where they were, no one would know where they came from.

This stands in stark contrast to Jesus' constant description of the world around him in his sayings! Jesus is not to be imagined rolling and unrolling scrolls to learn about God. Instead, he found that "our life, exempt from public haunt, finds tongues in trees, books in the running brooks, sermons in stones, and good in everything," to quote Shakespeare.[103]

Christian scholars over the past half century have gone through the Dead Sea Scrolls minutely, trying to find every bit of information they could to clarify the New Testament. The scholarly literature is immense—whole books have been filled with just bibliographies of publications on the Dead Sea Scrolls! One could expect this dramatic discovery of Jewish texts composed around Jesus' time to be very similar to what Jesus taught, especially since Jesus too was thought to have expected the world to come to an end very soon.

Of course there were obvious differences, which have tended to be played down. Jesus was a Galilean, and the Dead Sea Scrolls come from Judea. And the monks in the monastery who wrote them were—or had been—of the priestly class in Jerusalem, whereas Jesus was a layperson. They were scholars, whereas Jesus was only a blue-collar worker from a small hamlet in Galilee.

Compared to the enormous output of scholarship over the past half century, the results for explaining Jesus have been surprisingly meager. We should of course be very grateful for every bit of information they provide, all the more so because so little written information about Jesus' world was previously available in Jewish texts of the period. But the findings also should not be exaggerated, which has always been the temptation with new discoveries, especially on the part of those involved in publishing them.

Perhaps the most important result of half a century of research on the Dead Sea Scrolls in relation to Jesus is what is rarely admitted, since it cuts against the grain of what was hoped for: the scrolls are not very much like the teachings of Jesus, especially where it counts. This calls for some explanation.

Jesus was not a trained theologian, and so did not have a "system" of thought or develop key doctrines, much in contrast to someone like Paul—and much in contrast to the writers of the Dead Sea Scrolls! Jesus' sayings are, however, dominated by two idioms that have engrossed the attention of scholars: the "son of man" and the "kingdom of God." Jesus never defined either term; his failure to do so is explained by assuming they were concepts so common in that day that they called for no explanation—everybody was familiar enough with them to know what they meant! All he needed to say was that he was the son of man and that the kingdom of God was near, and everyone would have understood and become appropriately excited. But neither term plays an important role in the Dead Sea Scrolls! They obviously were not part of the very common theological terminology of the day that everybody understood.

What is even worse, the monks at the monastery who wrote the Dead Sea Scrolls expected the end of the world, the restoration of God's rule, and the coming of the Messiah in the very near future. If the idiom "kingdom of God" referred to the rule of God following the imminent end of the world and the idiom "son of man" referred to the Messiah who was about to come, then the Dead Sea Scrolls should be using this terminology all the time. The sect consisted of ardent believers that God was about to come and reign, along with the Messiah (or even two Messiahs!). They thought they were about to overthrow the corrupt priesthood (not to speak of the army of occupation) in the immediate future—they even had a scroll describing their triumphant victory in the final battle!

Since both key idioms, "kingdom of God" and "son of man," are largely absent from the Dead Sea sectarians' expectation of the end of the world that they were sure was about to happen, one may well wonder whether "kingdom of God" and "son of man" really are key terms pointing to the near end of the world on the part of Jesus. Does this mean that Jesus, though using these idioms in his message, was not focusing on the hope/threat that the world was about to come to its end? Could he, in this regard, have departed from his mentor, John the Baptist (though John also did not use these idioms in his predictions of the near end of the world)? We will have to see where the evidence points, when we get to these topics (in Chapters 5–8).

One sensationalist claim about the Dead Sea Scrolls that has gotten a lot of attention in the media may need to be debunked here, since it has been decisively rejected by the academic community. Let me express all due apologies for bothering you with it if you have not run across it. But if you have, and it has bothered you, let me help you out. (If, however, you want to skip it, just proceed on to the next section.)

Jesus' brother James was referred to in some early Christian texts as "James the Just"[104] in view of his great piety in leading the church in Jerusalem for a generation after Jesus' death. The founder of the Dead Sea sect is referred to in the scrolls as the "Teacher of Righteousness." Since Semitic languages are short on adjectives, they use prepositional phrases instead, so "of righteousness" means no more than "righteous," and of course "righteous" is a synonym for "just." So the Dead Sea sect was founded by someone whose name is unknown but who was referred to as "the Just Teacher." With no more to go on than this parallel, the impossible theory was launched that the Dead Sea sect was founded by Jesus' brother James the Just.

Impossible—for the Dead Sea sect was founded two centuries before Jesus! To make this wild theory work, the potsherds found in the ruins of the monastery would have to be dated two centuries later than they currently are. But the dating of pottery has become a real science in its own right, with accurate dating to within fifty years. Furthermore, the handwriting of the oldest scrolls would have to be dated two centuries later than they are, to bring them down to the time of Jesus and his brother James. But the dating of handwriting has also become a science that can pinpoint a handwriting to within half a century. A scholar cannot undo the sciences of dating pottery and dating handwriting just to fit a pet theory!

Why a pet theory? To disgrace the church! If Jesus' brother taught the same strict adherence to Jewish Law insisted on in the Dead Sea Scrolls, Jesus himself must have done so as well, in which case the gentile Christian church is way off base and should call it quits!

Thousands of small fragments found in Cave 4 of the Dead Sea sect still are not published. So the same Jewish scholar who had come up with the wild theory about the scrolls launched the equally false theory that it was the Roman Catholic Church that was suppressing them, because those fragments would prove his impossible theory by producing texts identifying the Teacher of Righteousness with James the Just.

Actually, this mass of small fragments has gone unpublished for a much less sensational reason, not because the church holds them back—the church does not even control them to be able to do so, even if it wanted to (which it does not). The reason they are not published lies elsewhere, on a much more pedantic level.

It takes more time to publish fragments than to publish complete texts—you have to try to fill in the letters missing in the holes and the letters before and after the fragment begins and ends on each line, and then to identify what kind of text it is, and so forth. The small team of (Protestant as well as Catholic) scholars who first got control of the material could work centuries before getting them all published—and they were unwilling to break their monopoly on them and let the much broader field of scholars gain access to them. But this was not because of "dangerous" material they contained, but is just an instance of all too common scholarly selfishness.

The person who launched the theory blaming the Roman Catholic Church found a way to get, from Israel, a copy of the closely guarded photographs of the unpublished fragments. But he himself was not a good enough scholar to read the fragments in order to find the evidence he wanted. So he decided, instead, to publish the pictures themselves, thereby making a name for himself and hoping others would help once the photographs were accessible to all. But he also did not know how to get his photographs of thousands of fragments published.

At this juncture, he turned to me, knowing I had functioned as the Permanent Secretary of UNESCO's International Committee for the Nag Hammadi Codices, which had broken the monopoly on these early Christian texts by publishing photographs of all of them. Although I (like all other scholars) disagreed with his far-fetched theory about the scrolls, I agreed to help publish the scroll fragments. So we published them in two big volumes in 1991, he hoping to prove his theory once they were read, I certain that their publication would put to rest that absurd theory. Over a decade has passed, and since no fragments supporting his theory have been found, the theory itself is fading into oblivion. May it rest in peace! And you may safely forget it.

JESUS FUNCTIONING AS A JEW

The Gospels in the New Testament are all documents of the gentile church, and hence do not go into great detail about the many Jewish practices of daily life to which Jesus of course conformed. Hence it is important to pay attention to the stories told about Jesus that do present him thinking and functioning as the Jew that he was. You can again and again see his point of departure in his Jewish culture. But then it is all the more striking to find him on occasion breaking through his own cultural traditions, when he feels a higher claim to do the right thing called for by the situation. Especially the Gospel of Mark, written for the gentile Christian church, points to Jesus' moving beyond the limitations of Jewish culture when he was a guest in a Jewish home:

> And as he sat at dinner in Levi's house, many tax collectors and sinners were also sitting with Jesus and his disciples—for there were many who followed him. When the scribes of the Pharisees saw that he was eating with sinners and tax collectors, they said to his disciples, "Why does he eat with tax collectors and sinners?" When Jesus heard this, he said to them, "Those who are well have no need of a physician, but those who are sick; I have come to call not the righteous but sinners."[105]

There is a rare instance of the Sayings Gospel Q and the Gospel of John sharing a story,[106] which hence must be very archaic. An officer in the Roman army of occupation stationed in Capernaum heard of Jesus as a faith healer, and so came to plead with him to heal his desperately sick boy. Jesus' reply was the surprised query:

> Am I, by coming, to heal him?[107]

This put-off has been so awkward to the gentile Christian church that the King James translation shifted it from a surprised question into a positive affirmation:

> I will come and heal him.[108]

Such a centurion stationed in Galilee knew quite well that a Jew would feel defiled by entering a gentile house. So he hastened to explain that Jesus did not actually have to enter his house to effect the cure of his boy, who lay there in bed. Jesus could just give an order for the boy to be healed, and the healing would take place! That is the way things are done in the military. An order is of course carried out, even if the officer giving the order is not actually present at the time. Jesus is impressed with the centurion's trust in the power of his word and makes the point that he has not found such faith in Israel. The boy is in fact healed.

Luke sensed that some special pleading would be in order if one expected a Jew to heal a Gentile. So he has a delegation of Jewish elders first come to Jesus to commend the centurion for having paid for the construction of a synagogue, thereby proving his love for the Jewish nation.[109] It was the same Luke who in Acts narrated in considerable detail the steps God took to persuade Peter to enter the house of another gentile centurion who also was generous to Jews.[110]

In a similar story, a Greek woman, a Syrophoenician by birth, that is, a Gentile,[111] called a Canaanite by Matthew,[112] brought her daughter to Jesus to be healed of demon possession. Here, as in the story of the centurion's boy, the Jewish sensibility is acknowledged by the Gentile, and yet the healing takes place. Jesus' first reply again reflects his Jewish heritage:

> Let the children be fed first, for it is not fair to take the children's food and throw it to the dogs.[113]

But when the mother implores him, pointing out that even the dogs get to eat the children's crumbs that fall from the table, he relents and heals the daughter.[114]

In their society, there was nothing worse than dogs, unless it was pigs, which were considered unclean. Jesus apparently has Gentiles in view in rejecting both:

> Do not give what is holy to dogs; and do not throw your pearls before pigs, or they will trample them under foot and turn and maul you.[115]

According to the Gospel of John, when Greeks want to see Jesus, they work through an intermediary, Philip, who in turn goes to Andrew; only then do the two of them approach Jesus, who welcomes this gentile interest as a very positive sign. But the Greeks, having thus launched Jesus into a lengthy discourse, promptly disappear from the story.[116]

It may be all too easy for us to focus on Jesus' gentile contacts that do take place and overlook his Jewish lifestyle that pervades his public ministry. So it may serve as a useful corrective to list here his use of the synagogue throughout his public ministry. He went habitually to the synagogues of Galilee to teach[117] and preach.[118] (Luke extends this to include Judea.[119]) Mark has the public ministry begin with the healing of a demon-possessed person in the synagogue at Capernaum, much to the congregation's amazement.[120] Luke has him begin his ministry with a sermon in the synagogue at Nazareth, which leads to a riot, from which he barely escapes alive.[121] Mark has him enter a synagogue and heal a man with a withered hand on the Sabbath. He defends this as an act of kindness permissible on the Sabbath, thereby motivating Pharisees who were present to conspire against him.[122] John has Jesus go, after the feeding of the five thousand, to the synagogue of Capernaum to explain at length that he is the bread of life.[123] The synagogue must have been a normal part of Jesus' public ministry.

Such Galilean synagogues may not have been separate buildings in their own right (of which no archaeological remains have been discovered for that period in Galilee), but homes used for synagogue services. But in any case they show Jesus functioning within the religion with which he grew up, in spite of having a new message and a new lifestyle. The Gospel of John has Jesus summarize his ministry quite appropriately:

> I have always taught in synagogues and in the temple, where all the Jews come together.[124]

We have already noted that in the Sayings Gospel Q Jesus is presented referring to Gentiles in a derogatory way, as well might have been common in Jewish villages.[125] Matthew betrays its Jewish Christian background by presenting even more such comments:

> And if you greet only your brothers and sisters, what more are you doing than others? Do not even the Gentiles do the same?

> When you are praying, do not heap up empty phrases as the Gentiles do; for they think that they will be heard because of their many words. Do not be like them.

> If the offender refuses to listen even to the church, let such a one be to you as a Gentile and a tax collector.[126]

Matthew even presents Jesus limiting his disciples' activities to Judaism:

> Do not go away on a road of the Gentiles, and enter no town of the Samaritans, but go rather to the lost sheep of the house of Israel.

> Truly I tell you, you will not have gone through all the towns of Israel before the son of man comes.[127]

After all, Matthew is the Gospel that goes back primarily to the Jewish Christian traditions of the Sayings Gospel Q—and only secondarily appropriates the Gospel of Mark, no doubt to gain entrance into the gentile church. But Luke was from its very inception more the Gospel of gentile Christian traditions.

Of course Jesus is portrayed as pronouncing woes on Jewish leaders such as Pharisees and exegetes of the Law.[128] Indeed, this negative portrayal is broadened to cover the present generation of Jews as heirs of those who persecuted the prophets.[129] It even applies to the Galilean towns where Jesus had worked but from which he was ultimately evicted.[130] Finally, this negativity is directed toward Jerusalem itself.[131]

But the reason this negativity is directed toward Jews is that it was to the Galilean Jews and to the Jerusalemites that Jesus and his followers had appealed in their intra-Jewish mission. As a result, it was by such Jewish audiences that they had been largely rejected. Jesus is constantly portrayed as debating with Jewish authorities, which is only additional documentation that he operated within Judaism, even while being its most severe critic.

THE GENTILE MISSION

The massive conversion of Gentiles to the Christian movement did not occur during Jesus' lifetime. It was left to Paul to find a way to accomplish that.

Barnabas, the first Christian philanthropist[132] and the head of the Christian mission in Antioch, had enlisted Paul's help, and together they created a church in Antioch that included a number of Gentiles.[133] They went to Jerusalem to seek approval. So they took with them a test case, Titus, who was a member of the Antioch church, though he was a Gentile, indeed an uncircumcised Greek.[134] They succeeded in convincing the Jewish Christian leaders in Jerusalem, Peter and James, that Titus was nonetheless a Christian. This led to the compromise of two missions, one to Jews led by Peter and one to Gentiles led by Paul.[135] By staying apart from the Gentiles, Christian Jews could retain their ceremonial purity without explicitly denying the Christian status of gentile Christians.

But when Paul and Barnabas were back at Antioch, this policy soon broke down. In practice the Antioch church, itself a mixed congregation, had come to permit table fellowship between Jews and Gentiles. The compromise reached in Jerusalem had apparently not envisioned the gentile church including Jewish Christians (except Paul and Barnabas), who of necessity would no longer be able to conform to the Jewish lifestyle in such matters as table fellowship. According to Jewish Law, such mingling with Gentiles would render a Jew unclean. Inevitably, in a mixed congregation the Jewish lifestyle would in practice come to be replaced by the gentile lifestyle. Paul and Barnabas themselves obviously accepted being classified as Gentiles when they ate with Gentiles:

> To the Jews I became as a Jew, in order to win Jews. To those under the Law I became as one under the Law (though I myself am not under the Law) so that I might win those under the Law. To those outside the Law I became as one outside the Law (though I am not free from God's law but am under Christ's law) so that I might win those outside the Law.[136]

Paul seems to have been aware that Jesus elevated love of neighbor to the highest commandment:

> For the whole Law is summed up in a single commandment, "You shall love your neighbor as yourself."[137]

Apparently for Paul this meant even if your neighbor is a Gentile—just as for Jesus it had meant even if your neighbor is a Samaritan! Paul's position recalls the story of Jesus and a Jewish legal authority agreeing over the greatest commandments, first to love God and second to love one's neighbor as oneself.[138] Thereupon the most Pauline Evangelist, Luke, continues the story with the legal authority posing the question: "And who is my neighbor?"[139] This Jewish legal authority would have known quite well that "neighbor" did not include just anybody. Indeed, the command to love one's neighbor was originally limited in its scope to one's own clan or ethnic group:

> With justice you shall judge your neighbor. You shall not go around as a slanderer among your people, and you shall not profit by the blood of your neighbor: I am the Lord. You shall not hate in your heart anyone of your kin; you shall reprove your neighbor, or you will incur guilt yourself. You shall not take vengeance or bear a grudge against any of your people, but you shall love your neighbor as yourself. I am the Lord.[140]

But Jesus answered the Jewish legal authority with the parable of the good Samaritan:

> A man was going down from Jerusalem to Jericho, and fell into the hands of robbers, who stripped him, beat him, and went away, leaving him half dead. Now by chance a priest was going down that road; and when he saw him, he passed by on the other side. So likewise a Levite, when he came to the place and saw him, passed by on the other side. But a Samaritan while traveling came near him; and when he saw him, he was moved with pity. He went to him and bandaged his wounds, having poured oil and wine on them. Then he put him on his own animal, brought him to an inn, and took care of him. The next day he took out two denarii, gave them to the innkeeper, and said, "Take care of him; and when I come back, I will repay you whatever more you spend." Which of these three, do you think, was a neighbor to the man who fell into the hands of the robbers?" He said,

"The one who showed him mercy." Jesus said to him, "Go and do likewise."[141]

Lest we in all smugness think that we do not need the example of the good Samaritan to know we should treat in a neighborly way anyone in need, let me give an illustration from our modern situation. I had the following painful experience in a local church some years ago, which I will never forget.

In effect, state law prohibited discrimination against potential house buyers on the basis of race or ethnicity. But a statewide referendum to revoke that law was put on the ballot, so that a house seller could pick and choose among potential buyers. The pastor of the local church was socially conscious and wanted the congregation to be as well, so he convened a meeting to discuss this referendum. A member of the congregation spoke on each side of the issue, and the floor was opened for discussion. An elderly woman rose to express her concern over the present law. She had lived in her house all her life and knew everyone up and down the street. She loved them all, just as Jesus had said she should love her neighbors. So she could not bring herself to sell her house to someone whom she knew they would not want among them. As a result, she favored repealing the law that would force her to sell to someone she knew her neighbors would not want on their street. She loved her neighbors, just as Jesus had said she should.

This so shocked me that I shall never get over it. It should make clear that much still needs to be done, even within the church.

Later on, Peter came to Antioch and did not himself make an issue of eating at the same table with gentile Christians. He may well have recalled the parable of the good Samaritan,[142] the healing of the Roman centurion's boy,[143] and the healing of the daughter of the gentile Syrophoenician woman.[144]

But then delegates came to Antioch from the Jerusalem church, which by that time was led by Jesus' brother James, who had not been a disciple of Jesus during his lifetime. When James's delegates arrived in Antioch, they abstained from the mixed table. Peter and even Barnabas felt obliged to go along, though both had up until then accepted the mixed table fellowship in Antioch.[145] One may recall that Peter himself had needed to be pushed into accepting his first Gentile convert, Cornelius,[146] and then Peter had to persuade the unwilling Christian Jews in Jerusalem to agree.[147] Obviously it was extremely difficult to break with the divinely sanctioned Jewish custom.

This latest turn of events in Antioch meant in practice that Christian Gentiles were excluded from fellowship with the more important Christian Jews. The status of Gentiles as Christians was thus put in question. At best, they would be second-class Christians. Paul vehemently argued against such an outcome,[148] but apparently he did not prevail. This may be inferred from the fact that he ultimately separated from Barnabas[149] and the Antioch church and went on missionary trips with other colleagues, supported by other congregations.

Yet Paul did honor his commitment to the Jerusalem church to provide funds for the poor there.[150] The reference to Jerusalem Christians as "the poor" no doubt did fit their economic status—the Jesus movement consisted largely of poor people, and the move to Jerusalem clearly did not improve the ability of Galilean fishermen,[151] who had made a living on the Sea of Galilee, to earn a living. (Paul, a tentmaker, could take his business with him.[152])

The ultimate separation of Paul from Barnabas and from the church in Antioch was the result of his rationale for including noncircumcised Gentiles into full standing in the church. Since even Jewish Christians who continued their Jewish lifestyle did not conform perfectly to Jewish Law, they were hardly in a different situation from "gentile sinners."[153] He pointed out:

Once again I testify to every man who lets himself be cir-
cumcised that he is obliged to obey the entire law.[154]

Since this is in practice impossible, Paul trivialized the Jewish
lifestyle:

For in Christ Jesus neither circumcision nor uncircumcision
counts for anything; the only thing that counts is faith
working through love.[155]

For Paul, this faith attests to the crucifixion of Jesus as a blood
sacrifice canceling out the sins of believers. In antiquity, and still
at that time in the temple at Jerusalem, animal sacrifice was
thought to effect forgiveness. But we no longer think that way
today.

It is ironic that Jesus himself, in the parable of the prodigal
son, told of a boy who had left home, squandered his inheritance
on a very bad lifestyle, and then in desperation returned remorsefully to his father, whereupon the father welcomed him back with
open arms. Jesus' God apparently did not need blood sacrifice to
make up for all the bad things the prodigal son had done, much to
the dismay of the prodigal son's self-righteous older brother,
though of course the fatted calf did lose its life in the process.[156]

Paul on the other hand repudiated those who could not make
sense of Jesus' horrible death as a blood sacrifice:

. . . the one who gave himself on behalf of our sins.[157]

Paul's focus on that blood sacrifice as necessary for salvation is
clear:

I determined not to know anything among you except Jesus
Christ and him crucified.[158]

A Christian missionary who had brought someone into the church, even Paul himself, deserved no credit for participating in that person's salvation, for nothing saves except Jesus' death:

Was Paul crucified for you?[159]

The gentile Christian church, from then until now, has been a religion built around the cross as its primary symbol and Holy Week, culminating in Good Friday and Easter, as its central religious ceremony. The outcome has been the Apostles' Creed, which omits completely Jesus' Galilean ministry as a Jew in defining who Jesus was and what he did that is worth believing. It is this glaring omission in our understanding of Jesus that the present book is seeking to fill.

———◆———

FOUR

WHAT WE DO AND DO NOT KNOW ABOUT JESUS

Especially over the past generation, during my lifetime, the quest of the historical Jesus has been renewed by valuable new tools that have become available. As a result, we know a lot more about Jesus' world than did previous generations. The actual circumstances of Galilee under Roman rule and the social structures against which Jesus' lifestyle and parables make sense have been brought increasingly into view: the exploitation of the native population, the patronage system used by those who wanted to get ahead, the abysmal economic status of a peasantry taxed into poverty, the Aramaic spoken by the Jewish population, the Greek spoken by the more cosmopolitan elite, and the low level of literacy in the Roman Empire.

There is even the unexpected information found in the ruins of ancient sites unearthed literally by dirt archeology. I myself have participated in excavations in Jordan by the Dead Sea, in Syria where the Ras Shamra clay tablets were discovered, on Cyprus at Enkomi, in Egypt at the site of the discovery of the Nag

Hammadi Codices, and indeed in Jesus' retreat center Bethsaida, and so I know firsthand about the importance of such digs.

Furthermore, very important manuscript discoveries made half a century ago have now been studied in great detail. The Dead Sea Scrolls were found at the Wadi Qumran overlooking the Dead Sea. They contain, as we have seen, a great many texts written in Hebrew by Jewish scholars around the time of Jesus. And the Nag Hammadi Codices were found in Upper Egypt at the foot of the Jabal at-Tarif, the cliff overlooking the Nile valley. They contain many offbeat early Christian texts, the best known of which is the *Gospel of Thomas.*

I have gone to considerable effort to break monopolies on both of these manuscript discoveries, monopolies held by the few scholars who got control of each of them early on. Not only did I publish a massive two-volume edition of the photographs of the unpublished Dead Sea Scroll fragments; I published for UNESCO an eleven-volume edition of photographs of the Nag Hammadi Codices, along with an English translation.

All these tools help to improve our understanding of Jesus. But it is his message, his point, his gospel, that is the focus of the present book. If thus the context into which Jesus is to be placed has become much more nuanced and reliable, the Jesus placed in that context nonetheless tends to be increasingly lost from sight in this mass of circumstantial evidence.

Of course, we know we cannot take him out of his world and transplant him into our own, lest we make him into what he was not. He did not know of the existence of the New World; he did not know astronomy, but at most astrology; he did not anticipate the Middle Ages, the Renaissance, the Enlightenment, the industrial revolution, the information age. He really was a first-century Galilean Jew. Hence, he did not address directly the issues of major importance to us, at least not in the language of our own cultural context. To us, he was not even politically correct. But we had been warned some time ago to avoid the "peril of modernizing Jesus." He was what he was as a first-century Galilean Jew.

Thus the present book does not ignore all the useful, indeed indispensable, new information surrounding Jesus that has become available during my lifetime. As a matter of fact, I have been deeply involved in most of it. But I have reached the point where I ask: So what? In this book I finally want to get to the point. What did Jesus himself have to say, and what was he actually up to?

In order to get what Jesus had to say into focus, we have to weed out what some would like to ascribe to him, even when it cannot be known. In most cases such guesses are probably inaccurate. In any case, they distract from what was of importance to Jesus. Hence, to get to that, they must first be put to one side.

JESUS' UNKNOWN CHILDHOOD AND YOUTH

We know that Jesus grew up in a small hamlet of Galilee, Nazareth (spelled Nazara in Q') — but nothing is known about Jesus' childhood and early manhood there! What childhood games did he play? Who were his childhood playmates? What did he do with his time?

More of our ignorance: Was there a synagogue in Nazareth that Jesus attended? If so, was there a school attached to it where boys could learn to read Hebrew? So could he read the Hebrew scriptures, though Aramaic was his mother tongue? How familiar was he with the Greek of the cultural elite and probably of the army of occupation?

What did Jesus look like when he grew up? The portraits of Jesus we all can recognize as Jesus are based more on classical portraits of Socrates, with whom Jesus was later compared, than on any information about Jesus' own appearance, which is completely unknown. When most people think of Jesus, they probably think of the European face ringed with blond hair with which we are all familiar, but which has nothing at all to do with Jesus' actual appearance.

What did he do as a young man? Did he have a social life? What kind of work did he do as a "carpenter"? What kind of relationship was there between father and son, both carpenters? Is the translation "carpenter" actually accurate, or is it somewhat misleading about the actual blue-collar work they did? Were they employed by the Romans in the rebuilding of nearby Sepphoris, as has often been speculated?

Actually, if we could light upon a wealth of information about Jesus as a young Galilean, it might do no more than document the pervasive extent to which Jesus shared the lack of knowledge, indeed much of the misinformation, of his day and age. Such new information might make us think of him as hopelessly dated, a child of his times, and no longer of relevance—which would be missing the point! Or, more likely, new information about Jesus might confirm our assumption that he was a very nice guy—but that is also not the point! He had something to say and wanted to be heard—his *gospel* is the point.

JESUS' FAMILY

What kind of family life did Jesus have when he was growing up? What kind of parents were Joseph and Mary? Even though we know no details of the home life in Nazareth, why not give Joseph and Mary credit by a sort of process of elimination? After all, their other son James seems to have turned out well—he ended up at the head of the Jerusalem church, and legend has it that he developed carbuncles on his knees from kneeling so long in the temple in prayer. He came to be called James the Just. The children must have been given a good upbringing. But that is only an inference from such meager reports.

Jesus was of course brought into his "public ministry" through the influence of John the Baptist (see Chapter 5). But what he did in his public ministry seems not to have been what John taught him to do, since their actual practice varied widely. John stayed at his baptizing location along the Jordan River performing his initiation rite, but Jesus soon left him, preferring to go door to door, hamlet to hamlet, across Galilee, trying to put into actual practice the kingdom of God (see Chapter 6). So what he actually did and what he told his followers to do must have come from somewhere other than John as his role model.

Yet the sparse information about family during the time of Jesus' public ministry suggests that there was no family involvement in his ministry, though in the early church his brothers James and Judas gained prominence. There are only very brief references to his siblings in the Gospels: James, Joseph, Judas, and Simon, plus several unnamed sisters.[2] They did not join him in his ministry, for they did not believe in him.[3] Actually, his family thought he was "beside himself" and, embarrassed, came to take him away to get him out of sight.[4] He in turn repudiated them.[5] Furthermore, on a visit to Nazareth, Jesus is reported to have said somewhat bitterly:

Prophets are not without honor, except in their hometown, and among their own kin, and in their own house.[6]

In the Gospel of John, Jesus attends a wedding at Cana in Galilee at which his mother is present.[7] When she tells him there is no wine left, his response seems a bit distant:

O woman, what have you to do with me? My hour has not yet come.[8]

Mary and her unnamed sister are among the other women at the crucifixion.[9] But it is odd that at the crucifixion Jesus is reported to have entrusted his mother not to a family member, but to the beloved disciple.[10] Yet Mary and Jesus' brothers are said to be with the disciples in Jerusalem after the crucifixion.[11] Of course, part of the problem is that such disparate reports from various Evangelists cannot really be reconciled into a thoroughly plausible reconstruction of the actual facts.

Paul reports a resurrection appearance to James in the authoritative list of appearances:

> Then he appeared to James, and afterwards to all the apostles.[12]

On an early trip to Jerusalem Paul says he saw James:

> Three years later I did go up to Jerusalem to get to know Cephas. I stayed with him for a fortnight, without seeing any other of the apostles, except James the Lord's brother.[13]

Paul mentions that "the rest of the apostles and the Lord's brothers, and Cephas" take their wives with them on the expense account,[14] thus recognizing that Jesus' brothers were among the Christian leaders.

Two of the brothers, James and Judas, became widely recognized as Christian leaders. The *Gospel of Thomas* ascribes a leading role to James:

> The disciples said to Jesus: "We know that you will depart from us. Who (then) will rule over us?" Jesus said to them: "No matter where you came from, you should go to James the Just, for whose sake heaven and earth came into being."[15]

The *Gospel of Thomas* then goes on to award the highest position, above Simon Peter and Matthew, to Judas.[16]

Though they did not actually compose written documents, texts were ascribed to James and Judas, so as to enhance the authority of such works, especially among Jewish Christians. The Letter of James in the New Testament and three texts in the Nag Hammadi Codices claim James as the author.[17]

Judas is credited with the Letter of Jude in the New Testament (though the King James translation avoided the full spelling "Judas" and preferred "Jude," to avoid an obvious confusion). Two of the Nag Hammadi texts are also ascribed to him,[18] though they too prefer to avoid a simple "Judas" and instead use what seems to have been his nickname, "Twin" (in Greek, Didymus; and in Aramaic, Thomas). The *Gospel of Thomas* begins: "These are the hidden words that Jesus spoke and I, Judas Didymus Thomas, wrote," and saying 13, cited above, refers to him as Thomas. The *Book of Thomas* begins by arguing that Thomas must know the truth about Jesus, since they are twins, or, as we might put it, have the same genes.[19]

All this may be stretching things a bit. But what is important to remember is that they grew up in the same home. Their parents, Joseph and Mary, should be given credit for raising fine children.

JESUS' EDUCATION ABROAD

Luke reports that as a boy of twelve Jesus' parents took him to Jerusalem, and that at the age of thirty he began his Galilean ministry.[20] The intervening eighteen years have fascinated people ever since, and their fantasy has at times gone wild over these "hidden years." It used to be common to imagine Jesus going to the sages of antiquity to gain the wisdom he supposedly could not have gained in Nazareth. So where else would one seek a guru other than in India? Even before much was known about its religions, Hinduism and Buddhism, at least it was known that the wise men came "from the East."[21]

But when Jesus' sayings are actually compared with what we now know of the centers of wisdom of his day, it turns out that no apparent influence can be detected. There is no reason to doubt that Jesus grew up in and around the carpenter's shop of his father at Nazareth.

JESUS' COMPLETELY UNKNOWN SEX LIFE, IF ANY

In more recent times, we have been less intrigued with Jesus' wisdom than with his sex life, about which we, however, know absolutely nothing. It is especially Mary Magdalene whom we have exploited for this purpose. And so, with all due apology to more sober readers, this sensationalism about her must first be replaced by a more accurate assessment of her important role in Jesus' public ministry, before we can move forward to present what we do know about Jesus.

Luke reports that Mary Magdalene is one of the "women who had been healed of evil spirits and infirmities," the one "from whom seven demons had gone out."[22] Unfortunately, Luke provides this bit of information immediately after his story of an anonymous woman of the street. When Jesus was having dinner at a Pharisee's house in Galilee, this woman came to Jesus with "an alabaster flask of ointment":

> Standing behind him at his feet, weeping, she began to wet his feet with her tears, and wiped them with the hair of her head, and kissed his feet, and anointed them with the ointment.[23]

This woman immediately disappears completely from the story, and yet the mention of this kind of bodily contact has been too much for some to let pass. The result has been that, down through the ages, Mary Magdalene has been falsely identified with this repentant prostitute, especially after this identification was officially proclaimed by Pope Gregory I in the sixth century.

This view received all too faint support from the fact that a similar story is told in the Gospel of John about another woman named Mary. But this is a completely different Mary, in this case the sister of Lazarus and Martha. It took place during a meal in their home in Bethany, in Judea, not in Galilee.

> Mary took a pound of costly ointment of pure nard and anointed the feet of Jesus and wiped his feet with her hair; and the house was filled with the fragrance of the ointment.

> It was Mary who anointed the Lord with ointment and wiped his feet with her hair, whose brother Lazarus was ill.[24]

Although the identification of Mary Magdalene with the woman of the street has finally been officially repudiated by the Roman Catholic Church at the Second Vatican Council, Mary Magdalene's own completely unknown sex life has become today the most popular (and lucrative) way to fantasize about Jesus' sex life. Absolutely nothing is known about the sex life of either, much less about a sexual relationship between them. To be quite blunt, this says more about the sex life (or lack of same) of those who participate in this fantasy than it does about Mary Magdalene or Jesus.

THE REAL MARY MAGDALENE

What do we know about the real Mary Magdalene? She was named after her hometown. The name of her town, Magdala, produced the term Magdalene, just as the town Gadara produced Gadarene,[25] and Nazara[26] produced Nazarene.[27]

Women in that day were usually named after the dominant male in their life, such as the father or husband: "Joanna wife of Chusa, Herod's steward,"[28] "Mary (mother) of James the younger and of Joses,"[29] Mary the (wife) of Clopas,"[30] "Mary the mother of John called Mark."[31] But among Jesus' female supporters, Susanna[32] and Salome[33] lack any such identification. To be sure, Matthew replaces Mark's reference to Salome with "the mother of the sons of Zebedee."[34]

Apparently Mary Magdalene had no such dominant male relative(s) after whom she was named, as the use of the name of her village to identify her might suggest. Or she may have lost her family identity on being abandoned due to her severe emotional condition or when she became a follower of Jesus. (The lonely, indeed isolated, Gerasene demoniac "lived among the tombs."[35] After Jesus healed him he wanted to follow Jesus,[36] but Jesus told him to "go home to your own."[37])

Mary Magdalene is part of the larger entourage of women accompanying Jesus and supporting his itinerant ministry as best they could. In this connection Luke cites her first in a list that continues:

> . . . and Joanna, the wife of Chusa, Herod's steward, and Susanna, and many others, who provided for them out of their means.[38]

She is mentioned more than any other, and indeed twice in first place, among the "many" women who accompanied Jesus.[39]

From all these references to Mary Magdalene, it is clear that she was preeminent among the women accompanying Jesus and his male disciples, down to the very end. Since women were considered no threat to the system, they were permitted to witness and bewail the execution of their loved ones. And here it is that

Mary Magdalene stands out so prominently, for she is among the women who witnessed the crucifixion:

> There were also women looking on from afar, among whom were Mary Magdalene, and Mary the mother of James the younger and of Joses, and Salome, who, when he was in Galilee, followed him, and ministered to him; and also many other women who came up with him to Jerusalem.

> But standing by the cross of Jesus were his mother, and his mother's sister, Mary the wife of Clopas, and Mary Magdalene.[40]

Male members of Jesus' entourage would automatically have been suspect to the Romans, as indeed was the case with Peter in the courtyard of the high priest:

> "You also were with the Nazarene, Jesus."

> "This man is one of them."

> "Certainly you are one of them; for you are a Galilean."[41]

Peter tucked his tail between his legs and got out alive by denying Jesus three times, whereupon the cock crowed, as Jesus had predicted when Peter had bragged he would be faithful to the bitter end.[42]

The women are reported to have been present even after the crucifixion:

> Mary Magdalene and Mary the mother of Joses saw where he was laid.[43]

In the story they go to the tomb to perform the burial rites usually entrusted to women:

> And when the Sabbath was past, Mary Magdalene, Mary the mother of James, and Salome brought spices, so that they might go and anoint him.[44]

The story relates that, much to their amazement, they found the tomb empty. But they saw a young man dressed in a white robe (according to Mark[45]), or an angel (according to Matthew[46]), or two men in dazzling apparel (according to Luke[47]), who told them that Jesus had risen from the dead. They were commissioned, in a formula familiar from the Old Testament:

> But go, tell his disciples and Peter that he is going before you to Galilee; there you will see him, as he told you.[48]

Mark concludes his Gospel with the report that the women were scared to tell the male disciples,[49] but this seems unfair to Luke, who held the apostles responsible:

> Now it was Mary Magdalene and Joanna and Mary the mother of James and the other women with them who told this to the apostles, but these words seemed to them an idle tale, and they did not believe them.[50]

It is the Gospel of John that at this point becomes the most important text for the role of Mary Magdalene. John says Mary Magdalene came alone to the tomb before dawn.[51] On finding the stone that closed it rolled away, she ran and told Peter and the beloved disciple, who raced to the tomb, saw it to be empty, and simply returned to their residences.[52] But Mary Magdalene stayed at the tomb:

But Mary stood weeping outside the tomb, and as she wept she stooped to look into the tomb; and she saw two angels in white, sitting where the body of Jesus had lain, one at the head and one at the feet. They said to her, "Woman, why are you weeping?" She said to them, "Because they have taken away my Lord, and I do not know where they have laid him." Saying this, she turned around and saw Jesus standing, but she did not know that it was Jesus. Jesus said to her, "Woman, why are you weeping? Whom do you seek?" Supposing him to be the gardener, she said to him, "Sir, if you have carried him away, tell me where you have laid him, and I will take him away." Jesus said to her, "Mary." She turned and said to him in Hebrew (actually Aramaic), "Rabbouni!"—which means Teacher. Jesus said to her, "Do not hold me, for I have not yet ascended to the Father; but go to my brethren and say to them, I am ascending to my Father and your Father, to my God and your God." Mary Magdalene went and said to the disciples, "I have seen the Lord."[53]

In order to bring Mark up to date with the Gospel of John, a later scribe added a text, which, since it was a later insertion, is no longer printed as part of the Bible, though it was in the copy used for the King James translation and so is included in that version:

Now when he rose early on the first day of the week, he appeared first to Mary Magdalene, from whom he had cast out seven demons.[54]

If in fact the male disciples fled for their lives, rather than being present at the crucifixion, whatever information we have about what actually went on would have to have come from the female disciples.

Of course some elements of the passion narrative may be based on the Old Testament, which the Evangelists would readily have accepted as a source of information about the crucifixion, for example, casting lots over Jesus' clothing:

> And they crucified him, and divided his clothes among them, casting lots to decide what each should take.[55]

From Psalms compare:

> They divide my clothes among themselves, and for my clothing they cast lots.[56]

In any case, the preeminent role of Mary Magdalene among the female disciples of Jesus is made quite clear in the Gospels.

Yet any romantic overtones one wishes to find in these references to her have to be read into the text and probably say more about the one who hears such overtones than about Mary Magdalene herself. Jesus functioned in his society as a "holy man," and no doubt was treated as such—hands off!

Of course anything is possible. But the historian's task is not to list the infinite number of possibilities and leave it to individuals to pick out the ones they prefer to elevate to what they consider to be "facts." Rather, it is the historian's responsibility to sort through them and identify those that, on the basis of the historical evidence, are to be considered probabilities. This is why no historian has given Mary Magdalene a romantic role in the "silent years" of Jesus' youth or thereafter. It has been quasi-historians, really novelists, who have not been able to resist the sensationalism inherent in such a story. So we need to consider soberly the probabilities concerning Mary.

Mary came from a small fishing village on the northwest shore of the Sea of Galilee. This was quite near—only a short sailboat ride—to the larger town at the northern tip of the Sea of Galilee, Capernaum, where Jesus had his base camp during his Galilean ministry. It is therefore quite reasonable to assume that he did have contact with her, that he did in fact heal her of the emotional affliction they understood as demon possession, and that she in turn did become a disciple.

But it is not probable at all that he would have had any occasion to come in contact with her while he was growing up as a young man in Nazareth, which was a hamlet in the hill country of Lower Galilee, not on the Sea of Galilee near Gadara, but considerably farther away. Nor is there any reason to assume he functioned as an exorcist to cure her of her emotional disorder before his conversion by John the Baptist.

It has been argued from silence that he must have married, since all Jewish men were supposed to be married by the time they reached the age of thirty. But that was often not the case— one need only think of Paul, John the Baptist, the monks living at Qumran who copied out the Dead Sea Scrolls, and so forth. So that notion cannot be elevated into a fact without any evidence.

After his baptism, Jesus returned to Nazareth just long enough to break with his family and move to Capernaum. His family came once to Capernaum to bring him home because he was "beside himself," crazy.[57] This of course raises a problem because the "holy family" is elsewhere presented as positive toward him. So the King James translation obscured this awkward reference to the family by translating the somewhat vague idiom meaning his family or relatives as "his friends."

This scene was already a problem for Matthew and Luke, who had of course glorified Jesus' parents in their infancy narratives, and so both simply left this verse out when they copied Mark. But Mark, after a story that puts the condition of being "beside himself" in theological language (exegetes of the Law accuse Jesus of being possessed by Beelzebul), resumes the story about his family:

> And his mother and his brothers came, and, standing outside, they sent to him and called him.[58]

He rebuffs them sharply:

> And looking around on those who sat about him, he said, "Here are my mother and my brothers! Whoever does the will of God is my brother, and sister, and mother."[59]

Such a denial of his biological kin can only be explained on the basis of the supreme role Jesus ascribed to his mission.

Jesus' rejection of family ties in favor of his mission is apparent from other references to family ties. Jesus turned down a potential disciple who wanted to honor his traditional family obligation:

> "Master, permit me first to go and bury my father." But he said to him: "Follow me, and leave the dead to bury their own dead."[60]

Jesus laid it on the line:

> For I have come to divide son against father, and daughter against her mother, and daughter-in-law against her mother-in-law.[61]

Similarly, he said:

> The one who does not hate father and mother cannot be my disciple; and the one who does not hate son and daughter cannot be my disciple.[62]

Luke includes in this list of rejected family relationships a reference to hating one's wife and children:

If any one comes to me and does not hate his own father
and mother and wife and children and brothers and sisters,
yes, and even his own life, he cannot be my disciple.[63]

Luke would hardly have quoted Jesus to this effect if Jesus had
been accompanied by a wife or "significant other."

Why is all this negative evidence never even mentioned by
those trying to make probable a romantic bond between Jesus
and Mary Magdalene, not to speak of their having raised children together (after Jesus revives from the crucifixion and they
move to the French Riviera), for which there is not the slightest
historical documentation? It is built on a late medieval legend,
no more.

In sum, the bare possibility that Jesus could have been married
is not supported by any existing first-century documentation,
which renders it highly improbable. The desire to create a prof-
itable sensation is more probably the basic motivation for making
such a claim.

MARY MAGDALENE IN LATER GOSPELS

Mary Magdalene is also prominent in Gospels of the last half of
the second century or later, which are less historically reliable,
however, given their late dates. Scholars over the years have never
used such late Gospels as reliable information about the historical
Jesus. But now, suddenly, these quite late Gospels are appealed to
for sensational information about his hidden sex life!

The *Gospel of Philip* (which of course was not written by Philip
the apostle, but by someone else a century after his death) reports
a close relation between Jesus and Mary Magdalene:

There were three women who always walked with the Lord:
Mary his mother, [his] sister, and the Magdalene, who is

called his companion. For Mary is his sister, and she is his mother, and she is his companion.[64]

Much has been made of this designation of Mary Magdalene as Jesus' companion, since this word can be used of a spouse as well as a business partner or fellow believer. But when the *Gospel of Philip* wants to refer to someone's wife, it always uses a different noun, a noun that only means wife.[65] This makes it very unlikely that the *Gospel of Philip* intends to designate Mary Magdalene as Jesus' wife by calling her his companion.

The *Gospel of Philip* also speaks of a kiss on the mouth:

> All who are born in the world are born of nature, and the others [are nourished] from where they are born. People [are] nourished from the promise of the heavenly place. [If they would be . . .] from the mouth, from which the word comes, they would be nourished from the mouth and would be perfect. The perfect conceive and give birth through a kiss. This is why we also kiss each other. We conceive from the grace within each other.[66]

In a fragmentary passage this kiss involves Mary Magdalene:

> As for Sophia who is called "the barren," she is the mother [of the] angels and the companion of the [. . .] Mary Magdalene[.] [. . . loved] her more than [all] the disciples [and used to] kiss her [often] on her [mouth]. The rest of [the disciples . . .]. They said to him: "Why do you love her more than all of us?" The savior answered and said to them: "Why do I not love you like her? When a blind person and one who sees are both together in darkness, they are no different from one another. When the light comes, then the

one who sees will see the light, and the one who is blind will remain in darkness."[67]

This passage clearly represents a reaction against the male chauvinism that had come to resent the privileged position of Mary Magdalene. It reflects a time in the church when women were struggling for an equal status among Christians, a status being challenged by males. This does not sound like the first-century Gospels, which do not present such male resistance to Mary Magdalene.

But the ritualistic kiss of peace is not to be taken as a euphemism for more explicitly sexual activity between Jesus and Mary Magdalene. The reference to kissing on the mouth is not a subtle reference to a "French kiss," but rather a doctrinal reference to the "word," the Gnostic message: "the mouth, from which the word comes."[68]

There is another instance in the Nag Hammadi Codices of Jesus kissing on the mouth (not to speak of a later Gnostic text in which Jesus and John the Baptist kiss each other[69]). Yet this instance, involving Jesus kissing his brother James, is almost never mentioned, since it does not have any pay dirt:

And he (Jesus) kissed my (James's) mouth. He took hold of me, saying, "My beloved! Behold, I shall reveal to you those (things) that (neither) [the] heavens nor their rulers have known."[70]

To be consistent and interpret these kisses as some would like to interpret the kiss of Jesus and Mary Magdalene, as sexual, causes a problem. Was Jesus homosexual? Or, to harmonize all the texts, was he bisexual? Of course no one would suggest such absurd interpretations! I mention them only to point out how absurd this

whole train of thought really is. A better solution is that, since it
is the post-resurrection Jesus who kisses James on the mouth, we
of course know that it cannot be sexual:

> For when they rise from the dead, they neither marry nor
> are given in marriage, but are like the angels in heaven.[71]

Another late-second-century Gospel, the *Gospel of Mary* (presumably Mary Magdalene), contains a similar resentment on the part
of Andrew and Peter about Mary's higher status:

> Peter said to Mary, "Sister, we know that the savior loved
> you more than the other women. Tell us the words of the
> savior that you remember, things you know but we do not
> because we have not heard them."[72]

Thereupon Mary answers in some detail, which leads to the following exchange:

> After Mary said these things, she was silent, since it was up
> to this point that the savior had spoken to her. Andrew re-
> sponded, addressing the brothers: "Say what you will about
> the things she has said, but I do not believe that the savior
> said these things, for indeed these teachings are strange
> ideas." Peter responded, bringing up similar concerns. He
> questioned them about the savior: "Did he really speak with
> a woman in private without our knowing about it? Are we
> to turn around and listen to her? Did he choose her over
> us?" Then Mary wept and said to Peter: "My brother Peter,
> what are you imagining? Do you think that I have thought
> up these things by myself in my heart or that I am telling
> lies about the savior?" Levi answered and said to Peter:
> "Peter, you have always been a wrathful person. Now I see

you contending against the woman like the adversaries. If the savior made her worthy, who are you to reject her? Surely the savior knows her very well. That is why he loved her more than us. Rather, we should be ashamed."[73]

Thus, when the *Gospel of Philip* and the *Gospel of Mary* were written, the male apostles led by Peter are presented as male chauvinists resentful of any eminence ascribed to Mary Magdalene. But this tells us more about these later times than about what happened in Jesus' time. The *Gospel of Philip* and the *Gospel of Mary* reveal quite clearly a feminist polemic against the male chauvinism that put down Mary Magdalene, and by implication women in general, which had come to expression more than a century after the events. When the Gospels of the New Testament were written, only half a century after the events, in the last thirty years of the first century, the eminent role of Mary Magdalene as well as of the other women was still fully acknowledged.

Whatever kissing was going on at the time of the *Gospel of Philip* and the *Gospel of Mary* was already rampant back in the time of Paul. He wrote a whole chapter full of greetings to his co-workers, listing them name after name, both men and women,[74] and in the middle of these greetings he wrote, "Greet one another with a holy kiss!"[75] He wrote the same thing once to the Thessalonians[76] and twice to the Corinthians.[77] And another New Testament Letter even concludes: "Greet one another with a kiss of love!"[78] Hadn't things really gotten out of hand from very early on?

No! For this has nothing to do with sex! It is what came to be known as the kiss of peace and is familiar in Christian liturgy down through the ages. In the local church I attend, it takes the form of the pastor calling upon the congregation to turn around and greet those seated nearby with a handshake and a greeting, "The peace of Christ be with you." Please—in my congregation these are not Sunday morning sex acts!

What is held against Mary Magdalene in the *Gospel of Philip* and the *Gospel of Mary* is no more than the outstanding role she played as a disciple in the Gospels. The later Gospels do not imply, must less divulge, any sexual tie with Jesus.

The rehabilitation of Mary Magdalene in modern times to her rightful place as Jesus' very loyal disciple, who stuck with him to the bitter end, should not be trivialized (or sensationalized) by projecting on her what may be no better than one's own sexual fantasies. One should not be carried away by the concepts of Jesus as the "bridegroom"[79] and the church as "the bride of Christ."[80]

FIVE

JESUS WAS CONVERTED BY JOHN

Jesus apparently grew up in Nazareth without a sense of calling, beyond the family's blue-collar job of carpentering, until he was some thirty years old.' Then he heard about a holy man who claimed that God was about to come down to earth to bring the evil society to an end and inaugurate God's own society. So people had begun to flock to him, to undergo his initiation rite, which symbolized putting off one's old life and beginning a new life that would gain admission to the new world. This rite involved being immersed by John in the Jordan River.

John lived an excessively ascetic life, doing nothing that depended on the evil society that was soon to come to an end, but living purely off what God provided in nature. John disdained the food and clothing typical of the society from which he had withdrawn. He lived off the land and, not wanting to be a nudist (as were some "holy men" of antiquity), he put together clothes from animal hair and skin:

> Now John was clothed with camel's hair, with a leather belt around his waist, and he ate locusts and wild honey.

For John came, neither eating nor drinking, and you say: "He has a demon!"[2]

John looked the part:

> What did you go out into the wilderness to look at? A reed shaken by the wind? If not, what did you go out to see? A person arrayed in finery? Look, those wearing finery are in kings' houses. But then what did you go out to see? A prophet? Yes, I tell you, even more than a prophet![3]

John was rejected by the authorities, who dismissed him without further ado (as he did the religious authorities!). But common people, who suffered the most from the evils of society, flocked to him hoping for the deliverance he promised.[4]

Jesus was one of those common people who went out to John. He obviously believed John's message, for he underwent John's rite of initiation symbolizing his message: that one should end one's life in the evil society and begin a new life for the new world. Since the Gospel of John locates this at "Bethany across the Jordan,"[5] the initiation rite may have been a matter of entering the Jordan on the far side and coming out in the "promised land." Jesus may well have taken off his clothes that identified him as part of the evil society, gone into the water naked, and come out ready to begin the new life. But when he came out of the water, Jesus did not dress as John did. He apparently resumed his normal garb, except that he went barefoot,[6] perhaps as a sign of penance.

JESUS' DIVERGENT PRACTICE

The difference between Jesus' clothing and John's is already an indication that Jesus did not automatically adopt John's lifestyle.

Furthermore, he did not literally become a follower in the sense of staying permanently with John. Rather, he left John, but apparently did not immediately go home. Instead, he went out into the wilderness alone for a time of inner turmoil and indecision known to us as his "temptation."[7]

Apparently he finally decided not to carry on a baptizing ministry like that of John at the Jordan, but rather to come to grips firsthand with the completely new life of those who had renounced attachment to the evil society His—and their—basic problem was this: After the renunciation of the normal lifestyle through immersion, how are you to carry on the new life as long as you are in a society that has not changed? John, by staying in the wilderness at the Jordan, did not really have to face that problem firsthand, but at most could give advice from afar:

Whoever has two coats must share with anyone who has none; and whoever has food must do likewise.[8]

But how does that function in practice?

Perhaps it is Jesus' wrestling with this question that the Sayings Gospel Q brings to expression as a debate with the devil in the three temptations of Jesus, to change stones into loaves, to throw himself down from the tip of the temple, and to bow down to the devil so as to be given all the kingdoms of the world. In any case, the temptations are the only thing that occurs in the Sayings Gospel Q between John's baptizing of Jesus and Jesus' launching of his own ministry with his inaugural "Sermon," for Jesus went directly to the people with the good news of a lifestyle underwritten by God himself—his "gospel," to which the present book is dedicated.

Jesus returned to Galilee,[9] which inevitably involved dependence on others for his livelihood. If John and those with him could scrounge food from the wilds of nature around them, Jesus inevitably counted on women to prepare food for him wherever he was given lodging.

Jesus first came home to Nazareth, where his message fell on deaf ears.[10] He learned the hard way that

> prophets are not without honor, except in their hometown, and among their own kin, and in their own house.[11]

He moved to Capernaum, on the northern shore of the Sea of Galilee, to launch there his own ministry.[12]

Accompanying Jesus' change of locale from that of John in the Jordan Valley was his not using John's rite of initiation, immersion. There is indeed a passing report in the Gospel of John that Jesus did baptize:

> John and his disciples went into the land of Judea; there he remained with them and baptized. . . . Jesus was making and baptizing more disciples than John . . . [13]

But this is immediately corrected:

> . . . although Jesus himself did not baptize, but only his disciples.[14]

Even one of the recently discovered early Christian Gnostic texts makes this quite clear:

> For the son of man did not baptize any of his disciples.[15]

Since there is no other reference even to his disciples baptizing during Jesus' lifetime, the Gospel of John's statement about his disciples baptizing is no doubt a reference to the baptismal practice initiated in Paul's time. Baptism may have been thought especially necessary for "gentile sinners."[16] But even Paul said:

> For Christ did not send me to baptize but to proclaim the gospel.[17]

According to Matthew, Jesus changed his policy of going only to the Jews after his resurrection, when he commissioned the apostles to go to the Gentiles and first in that context mentioned Christian baptism:

> Go therefore and make disciples of all nations, baptizing them in the name of the Father and of the Son and of the Holy Spirit . . .[18]

According to the Gospel of Luke, Christians distinguished their baptism from that of John by arguing that only theirs imparted the Holy Spirit.[19] This of course stands in some tension with the report of Jesus' baptism by John, according to which Jesus did receive the Spirit "like a dove."[20] But what the two reports have in common is the claim that the Holy Spirit is limited to Christians.[21]

In other regards as well, Jesus did not initially take over John's better-organized religious practices. Whereas John and his disciples fasted, Jesus' disciples did not fast until after his death.[22] According to Luke, Jesus taught his disciples what we know as the Lord's Prayer only when they complained to him that John had taught his disciples to pray and Jesus had not done so.[23] From such details one can infer that initially the religious practices of the Baptist movement were better organized than those of the Jesus movement. Jesus' untimely death may have come too soon for such organizational traits to have been developed.

JESUS' DIVERGENT MESSAGE

John's message was basically negative, apocalyptic. God would soon come and burn up the evil oppressors, so people needed to distance themselves immediately from such evil:

> Who warned you to run from the impending rage? So bear fruit worthy of repentance, and do not presume to tell yourselves: "We have as forefather Abraham!" For I tell you: God can produce children for Abraham right out of these rocks! And the ax already lies at the root of the trees. So every tree not bearing healthy fruit is to be chopped down and thrown on the fire.[24]

The focus of John's message seems to have been a last-chance warning before the imminent coming of God for the day of judgment.

Since Jesus was impressed enough by John's message to undergo John's initiation rite of immersion, it is easy to assume his message continued that of John. But there is a warning signal in the fact that Jesus' practice did diverge widely from that of John—food and clothing, the locale of his ministry, baptism as a rite of initiation, rituals such as fasting and prayer. Since practice and message tend to be correlated, there is good reason to think that Jesus' message would diverge from that of John just as much as did his practice.

When the messages are compared, such a divergence does in fact seem to be the case. John warned of the burning of the unproductive tree,[25] the baptism with windstorm and lightning,[26] the chaff burning in an unquenchable fire.[27] They are John's metaphors of judgment. But none of them recurs in Jesus' own message.

The contrast can be seen most clearly in the one instance in which John and Jesus seem to share a metaphor: every tree bears the kind of fruit that comes from the kind of tree it is. For John, this points to imminent judgment:

So every tree not bearing healthy fruit is to be chopped down and thrown on the fire.[28]

Jesus uses the same metaphor to make sage observations about living, without any reference to imminent judgment:

No healthy tree bears rotten fruit, nor on the other hand does a decayed tree bear healthy fruit. For from the fruit the tree is known. Are figs picked from thorns, or grapes from thistles? The good person from one's good treasure casts up good things, and the evil person from the evil treasure casts up evil things. For from exuberance of heart one's mouth speaks.[29]

Jesus once told a parable about a fig tree that had borne no fruit for three years and so was about to be cut down, until the vine-dresser pleaded for another year to fertilize it and make it produce fruit so that it could be saved.[30] But Mark has Jesus reproach the fig tree, even though it was not the fruit bearing season,[31] whereupon Matthew reports that the fig tree withered[32]—no doubt part of the vengeance characteristic of Matthew's editing elsewhere, a major departure from Jesus' own attitude.

It seems clear that Jesus' message, in sharp contrast to that of John, focused on life in the here and now, the reality of God reigning. What, in practice, does it mean, to end a life that participated in the evils of society and to begin a life in which it is God who is reigning? This is what Jesus was trying to work out in his own living and what his message called on his listeners to do:

Love your enemies and pray for those persecuting you, so
that you may become sons of your Father, for he raises his
sun on bad and good and rains on the just and unjust.

The one who slaps you on the cheek, offer him the other as
well; and to the person wanting to take you to court and get
your shirt, turn over to him the coat as well. And the one
who conscripts you for one mile, go with him a second. To
the one who asks of you, give; and from the one who borrows, do not ask back what is yours.[33]

Jesus' message continued to be delivered by his disciples, but
had less and less success. They were obviously less "charismatic."
The movement seemed to be dying out, especially with the passing of those who had heard Jesus himself. The disciples could
thus come to experience the generation after Jesus' death as an
"evil generation."[34] As a result, "this generation" became a designation for those whom God rejects.[35] Indeed, woes were pronounced on their leaders, the Pharisees[36] and exegetes of the
Law.[37]

Then came the Jewish war (66–70 C.E.), whose disastrous climax was the destruction of the magnificent temple Herod had
built in Jerusalem. The Jews of the day could only understand the
Romans' destruction of Herod's temple in the same way that the
Hebrew scriptures explained the destruction of Solomon's temple by the Babylonians more than half a millennium earlier (586
B.C.E.). It was not God who has broken his covenant with Israel—
perish the thought! It must be that Israel has broken its covenant
with God.

Jesus' surviving disciples, all of whom were Jews, would naturally have shared this Jewish sentiment, but focused it on their
own situation: The breaking of the covenant had consisted most
of all in rejecting Jesus' message, a rejection they understood as

the culmination of the rejecting of God's prophets down through the ages. The final editor of the Sayings Gospel Q actually quotes a text to this effect ascribed to Wisdom, Judaism's personification of God:

> Therefore also Wisdom said: "I will send them prophets and sages, and some of them they will kill and persecute, so that a settling of accounts for the blood of all the prophets poured out from the founding of the world may be required of this generation, from the blood of Abel to the blood of Zechariah, murdered between the sacrificial altar and the House." Yes, I tell you: An accounting will be required of this generation!
>
> "O Jerusalem, Jerusalem, who kills the prophets and stones those sent to her! How often I wanted to gather your children together, as a hen gathers her nestlings under her wings, and you were not willing! Look, your House is forsaken! I tell you: You will not see me until the time comes when you say: 'Blessed is the one who comes in the name of the Lord!'"[38]

The destruction of the temple in the year 70 seems to be envisaged here where the text speaks of the temple being "forsaken" by God, for otherwise God could be expected to protect his temple. So it would seem necessary for God each time to abandon his temple before it could be destroyed. Thus God revealed himself as a vengeful God by punishing Israel again with this second destruction of the temple. Jesus' sunny experience of God showering love even on the bad and unjust gave way to the grim experience of a God of vengeance.

The destruction of the temple, interpreted through scripture as a new devastating punishment by God, in effect replaced Jesus' revelation of God for the Q community. Accordingly, in the redaction of the Sayings Gospel Q. God no longer shines his sun and rains his showers also on the bad and unjust, but throws them

> out into the outer darkness, where there will be wailing and grinding of teeth.[39]

The Q community's final repudiation of Israel for rejecting the messages of John and Jesus thus came to expression in very negative language. Jesus' own commitment to loving even one's enemies, as does the Father in heaven, was replaced by a God who has the temple destroyed as punishment, if not of his enemies, then of his disobedient people.

There is surely a certain irony in the fact that Jesus discovered God in the sunshine and showers, but, as his disciples over the years became more learned in the scriptures, they lost sight of his revelation of God. Jesus had said quite simply:

> I praise you, Father, Lord of heaven and earth, for you hid these things from sages and the learned, and disclosed them to children.[40]

But in the judgmentalism characteristic of the final editing of the Sayings Gospel Q at the time of the Jewish war, there is no overlap in terminology with John's language predicting the imminent day of judgment. That is, there is no indication that such language on the part of John was carried over into the sayings spoken by Jesus, and then reused by his disciples at the time of the Jewish war. Rather, the language ascribed to John seems limited to the Baptist movement and was never ascribed to those in the Jesus movement. Therefore we cannot assume that Jesus' message was simply a continuation of that of John. It seems to have been distinctively new, with his gospel of the kingdom of God.

THE CHRISTIANIZING OF JOHN'S MESSAGE

John had predicted that God would come any moment to burn down the evil world with his traditional weapons of windstorm and lightning, which is apparently what is lurking behind Q's more Christian "holy Spirit and fire":

> I baptize you in water, but the one to come after me is more powerful than I, whose sandals I am not fit to take off. He will baptize you in holy Spirit and fire. His pitchfork is in his hand, and he will clear his threshing floor and gather the wheat into his granary, but the chaff he will burn on a fire that can never be put out.[41]

This apocalyptic "one to come" no doubt referred originally to God coming for the day of judgment, and this then needed to be Christianized to refer to Jesus.

To be sure, it has been argued that the reference to the "one to come" wearing sandals and having a pitchfork in his hand indicates that it is not God who is envisaged, but a human with feet and hands. This would make it possible to argue that John was in fact expecting a human like Jesus. Yet these are clearly metaphors not intended as a literal description of the "one to come," any more than is Jesus' reference to casting out demons "by the finger of God" meant literally.[42]

John's talk about the "one to come" in the language of natural disasters is of course hardly fitting as a description of what Jesus actually did. So the Sayings Gospel Q first of all simply made it fit what Jesus was actually doing:

> And John, on hearing about all these things, sending through his disciples, said to him: "Are you the one to come, or are we to expect someone else?" And in reply he

said to them: "Go report to John what you hear and see: The blind regain their sight and the lame walk around, the skin-diseased are cleansed and the deaf hear, and the dead are raised, and the poor are evangelized. And blessed is whoever is not offended by me."[43]

Then the Sayings Gospel Q transferred John's apocalyptic figure away from Jesus' public ministry in Galilee to refer to his coming at the day of judgment:

For as the lightning streaks out from Sunrise and flashes as far as Sunset, so will the son of humanity be on his day.[44]

In this way, the Sayings Gospel Q could use the expression about the "one to come" to refer to Jesus at the day of judgment, though the meaning (and hence the translation) is somewhat different:

You will not see me until the time comes when you say: "Blessed is the one who comes in the name of the Lord!"[45]

In this case what is usually translated the "one to come" is translated the "one who comes," for it involves the recitation of a familiar line from a psalm[46] used of pilgrims coming up to Jerusalem at Passover. In fact, it is so used by the canonical Gospels at the time of Jesus' "triumphal entry":

Hosanna! Blessed is the one who comes in the name of the Lord![47]

Then the rest of John's terrible prediction became, to the extent possible, also Christianized. The baptism that John predicted, with windstorm and lightning, became, in the Christian retelling, the holy Spirit and fire,[48] then just the Holy Spirit.[49] Thus, bit by bit, the Greek word used for windstorm, meaning "wind" or "spirit," became "holy," since the windstorm was done by God, from which ultimately emerged the Christian term "Holy Spirit."

Yet Luke, in telling the story of Pentecost, does seem to recall the original reference to windstorm and lightning as acts of God, which he too Christianizes by placing their fulfillment at Pentecost.

> And suddenly from heaven there came a sound like the rush of a violent wind, and it filled the entire house where they were sitting. Divided tongues, as of fire, appeared among them . . .[50]

This is then interpreted as the coming of the Holy Spirit and the gift of tongues at Pentecost, not as natural disasters done by God at the final judgment. John's message has become a Christian message.

THE CHRISTIANIZING OF JOHN

John the Baptist was so important in the Christian story that he too had somehow to be Christianized. The Gospel of John simply presents him as in effect the first Christian witness to Jesus:

> Here is the Lamb of God who takes away the sin of the world! . . . And I myself have seen and have testified that this is the Son of God. . . . Look, here is the Lamb of God! . . . I am not the Messiah, but I have been sent ahead of him.[51]

This is clearly a Christian retelling in order to include John in the fold and to take advantage of his endorsement of Jesus.

The Sayings Gospel Q devotes a surprising amount of attention to John. It contains the longest account of what John actually had to say,[52] also reports John's baptism of Jesus,[53] and later on presents a long segment analyzing the relation of John and Jesus.[54] In this segment on John and Jesus, the Sayings Gospel Q includes very high praise of John:

> Yes, I tell you, even more than a prophet! This is the one about whom it has been written: "Look, I am sending my messenger ahead of you, who will prepare your path in front of you." I tell you: There has not arisen among women's offspring anyone who surpasses John.[55]

The Sayings Gospel Q also reports that tax collectors and other outcasts responded positively to John (as they did to Jesus), whereas the religious authorities rejected him.[56] Also in this rejection John is put parallel to Jesus; both are rejected by "this generation," John as demon-possessed, in view of his extreme asceticism, and Jesus as a drunkard, in view of his both eating and drinking[57]—yet both are equally vindicated by divine Wisdom.[58]

But then the Sayings Gospel Q makes it painfully clear that John is, after all, inferior to Jesus and his disciples:

> Yet the least significant in God's kingdom is more than he.[59]

Already the original presentation of John's message had envisaged the "one to come" as superior to John, since, after all, it was a reference to God:

> The one to come after me is more powerful than I, whose sandals I am not fit to take off.[60]

Of course this makes perfect Baptist sense, so long as the "one to come" refers to God coming in judgment. But once it is interpreted to refer to Jesus, it becomes part of the argument to make Jesus superior to John.

Luke sensed the problem that Jesus' baptism by John seemed to suggest John's superiority, so he does his best to brush off this embarrassing detail. He periodizes the story so that Jesus' ministry is distinct from that of John, and does so by reporting John's imprisonment even before he mentions, only in passing, Jesus' baptism, without actually saying who baptized him. Someone who only read Luke would hardly imagine that it was John who baptized Jesus:

> But Herod the ruler, who had been rebuked by him (John) because of Herodias, his brother's wife, and because of all the evil things that Herod had done, added to them all by shutting up John in prison. Now when all the people were baptized, and when Jesus also had been baptized and was praying . . .[61]

Luke's downplaying of John is made clear in his presentation of Paul's sermon in the synagogue of Antioch in Pisidia. After narrating the history of Israel, the sermon goes on with the Christianized version of John's statement:

> Of this man's posterity God has brought to Israel a Savior, Jesus, as he promised; before his coming John had already proclaimed a baptism of repentance to all the people of Israel. And as John was finishing his work, he said, "What do you suppose that I am? I am not he. No, but one is coming after me; I am not worthy to untie the thong of his sandals on his feet."[62]

Matthew carries this argument for Jesus' superiority to John one step further by inserting John's self-effacing protest into the story of Jesus' baptism:

> John would have prevented him, saying: "I need to be baptized by you, and do you come to me?" But Jesus answered him, "Let it be so now, for it is fitting for us in this way to fulfill all righteousness."[63]

In fact, this whole discussion of John and Jesus in the Sayings Gospel Q is due to John's sending a delegation to Jesus to inquire if he is, as presumably was being claimed on the Christian side, the "one to come," whose coming John had announced as imminent. John's original language had indeed sounded as if he were announcing God's own coming in judgment, so it seems clear that John had not had Jesus in view (in spite of the Gospel of John maintaining the reverse). So the Baptists ask Jesus the pointed question:

> Are you the one to come, or are we to expect someone else?[64]

The answer one might expect, in view of John's prediction of an apocalyptic judge, would be to portray Jesus in just such terms. Instead, we have a very positive summary of Jesus' public ministry. It is based on a series of benevolent predictions scattered throughout the standard Greek translation of Isaiah, culminating in one prediction on which the Sayings Gospel Q's summary is primarily built:

> The Spirit of the Lord God is upon me, because the Lord has anointed me; he has sent me to evangelize the poor, to bind up the brokenhearted, to proclaim liberty to the captives, the recovery of sight to the blind.[65]

In the Sayings Gospel Q itself, Jesus is presented as answering John's delegates with the claim that he is indeed the "one to come," but as fulfilling Isaiah's good news rather than John's judgmentalism:

> The blind regain their sight and the lame walk around, the skin-diseased are cleansed and the deaf hear, and the dead are raised, and the poor are evangelized."

It seemed quite possible to argue that Jesus fulfilled such prophecies during his Galilean ministry, and so each of the Gospels that made use of the Sayings Gospel Q turned its energies in this direction.

The first major section of the Sayings Gospel Q,[67] about a third of its total length, seems to have been organized so as to support this claim. John's prediction of the "one to come" stands at the beginning,[68] the section reaches its climax when John's delegation asks Jesus if he really is that "one to come,"[69] and Jesus' positive reply follows.[70] The material intervening between the beginning and end of this first major section in the Sayings Gospel Q is intended to prove the case by documenting the fulfillment of Isaiah's prophecy. The Spirit came upon Jesus at his baptism,[71] the Sermon began "Blessed are you poor, for God's reign is for you,"[72] and the centurion's boy was healed.[73] Thus this intervening material in the Sayings Gospel Q serves to prepare John's delegation, or at least the readers of the Sayings Gospel Q, to accept at face value Jesus' claim to be the "one to come."

It may be relevant to note a side remark in the segment about John and Jesus. After the delegation from John has left, Jesus asks the surrounding crowd:

> What did you go out into the wilderness to look at?[74]

The following context makes it clear that the implicit answer is that they had gone out to see John. That is, Jesus' own listeners were devoted enough to John to have hiked out into the wilderness to see John! Apparently John and Jesus shared much the same constituency.

The segment about John and Jesus does not make clear, however, whether the audience that had gone out into the wilderness to see John had actually become Baptists. But on the other hand neither does it make clear whether the audience became Jesus' disciples. Perhaps this is too modern a question to ask—the audience may simply be meant to represent conscientious Jewish laity in general.

What is even more surprising is that the reaction of John's delegates to Jesus is not actually stated one way or the other. Jesus' concluding remark to them does not seem very promising:

Blessed is whoever is not offended by me.[75]

One would think the most useful thing the Sayings Gospel Q could have reported at this juncture would have been that John's disciples accepted the evidence at face value and promptly became disciples of Jesus. But since this helpful bit of information is not provided, we can only suspect that it did not happen. The cultivation of the Baptists was apparently still in progress as unfinished business.

Indeed, the evidence itself had not been adequately presented in the Sayings Gospel Q, for only one healing had actually been recorded to prove the validity of Q's list of four kinds of healings plus the resurrecting of the dead. After all, Q is a collection of sayings, not of healing stories! The one healing, namely, the healing of the centurion's boy,[76] is told in a way that documents less well Jesus as a powerful healer than as one with a powerful word. The point is made that Jesus effects the healing just by giving the command, without even entering the gentile house where the boy lay sick.[77] Since even here the nature of the illness is not given, the story does not document any one of the four kinds of illnesses listed in Jesus' reply, not to speak of the raising of the dead. Hence, it is not surprising that the evangelizing of the poor is in fact the only specific in Jesus' list that had already been well documented in the Sayings Gospel Q prior to the arrival of the delegates from John. The Sayings Gospel Q had initiated Jesus' ministry by quoting an early collection of Jesus' sayings, what we call the Sermon.[78]

Even Luke sensed the problem, and so, after narrating the arrival of the delegation from John, he thoughtfully inserts, just before Jesus gives them his reply:

> Jesus had just then cured many people of diseases, plagues, and evil spirits, and had given sight to many who were blind.[79]

The item with which this list concludes, the bestowing of sight, is the first in the list of healings in Jesus' reply: "The blind regain their sight." John's delegates could not have helped having a good first impression. But what of the climactic claim "the dead are raised"? Just before narrating Q's story of John sending his delegation, Luke reports that Jesus had in fact raised from the dead the son of the widow of Nain.[80] As a result of these Lukan additions, at least readers of Luke's Gospel are well disposed to concede that Jesus is the "one to come."

When the dwindling Q community finally merged into the booming gentile church, and so had to incorporate into its Sayings Gospel Q the gentile church's Gospel of Mark, the result seems to have been the production of the Gospel of Matthew. Here we can clearly observe Matthew's attempt to bring to completion Q's appeal to John's followers to join the Jesus movement. The Sayings

Gospel Q had only succeeded in pointing out that the Spirit had indeed descended upon Jesus at his baptism, the evangelization of the poor had taken place in the Sermon beginning "Blessed are you poor, for God's reign is for you," and one healing, of an unspecified illness, had taken place. But what could Matthew do with the list of specific healings, much less the resurrection of the dead, none of which have thus far been narrated in the Sayings Gospel Q?

Matthew expended even more effort than Luke to complete the argument, so as to have all the evidence in hand before narrating the story of John's disciples coming to ask if Jesus is the "one to come." To beef up the Sermon, Matthew simply inserted important clusters of archaic sayings available to him in the Sayings Gospel Q and in his other sources to produce what we now call the Sermon on the Mount (the "mount" having come to Matthew from Mark[81]). But to produce healing narratives comparable to the list in the Sayings Gospel Q, Matthew could not build primarily on Q, since the healings were not there—it is a sayings collection!

All the Sayings Gospel Q has to offer is a passing reference later on[82] to Jesus having "cast out a demon which made a person mute," whereupon the demon-possessed person speaks. Matthew reports this at its "right" position in Q sequence,[83] adding that the unfortunate person was also blind. But Matthew had already brought the same story forward in its original form (that is, without the addition of the blindness),[84] in order to use it prior to John's sending his delegates to Jesus. In this way the mute person is made to document in advance that "the deaf hear."

This calls for some explanation. People born deaf never learned to speak (prior to Helen Keller), and even if they became deaf only later in life, they could not follow the conversation and so had nothing to say. As a result, the Greek term used here literally means "dull," but serves to mean both "mute" and "deaf." Actually, this Greek word is usually used to refer to deafness, rather than dumbness, since there is another Greek word, literally "speech-less," that is usually used to refer to just dumbness. Perhaps the Greek word used by the Sayings Gospel Q could best be translated "deaf-mute," since it was used both for dull hearing and for the resultant dull speaking.

The point of this digression into the depths of the Greek language is to make clear that the same word is used in Jesus' reply to John's delegation that occurs here in the healing. If the expression in the reply to John's delegation, literally "the dull *hear*," leads us to translate "the *deaf* hear," in the healing story the reference to "the dull *speak*" leads one to translate "the *dumb* speak." But it is the same word in Greek in both cases. In sum, the distinction in English between *deaf* and *dumb* does not exist in this Greek word. So the story of the *deaf-mute* speaking documents equally well "the deaf hear" in the list of Jesus' healings.

Since there are no other healings in the Sayings Gospel Q, Matthew has to turn to his other source, the Gospel of Mark, which is full of healing narratives, to find the missing story of someone "regaining sight." He uses the story of a blind beggar called Bartimaeus, whom Jesus heals in Jericho on his way to Jerusalem.[85] On the one hand, Matthew does tell this story in its "right" (Markan) location in Jericho,[86] though omitting the identification of the person and even omitting the reference to him as a beggar, indeed telling the story as having to do with two such blind persons. But, on the other hand, he had already used it (also as two anonymous blind persons) near the opening of Jesus' Galilean ministry, between the Sermon on the Mount and John's sending his delegates to Jesus,[87] so that it could function to document "the blind regain their sight." Fortunately, the remaining two healings listed in response to John's inquiry were early enough in Mark that Matthew could leave them in their Markan position and still narrate them prior to the list of healings provided to John's delegates.[88]

But "the dead are raised" called for another rearrangement of Markan order. The story with which we are familiar under the title "the healing of Jairus's daughter"[89] concerns a twelve-year-old.[90] Her father, according to Mark, implored Jesus to come, saying, "My little daughter is at the point of death."[91] Matthew edits this into something he can use by having the father say, "My daughter has just died."[92] Thus this story comes to qualify as an instance of fulfilling the item in the list "the dead are raised," even though Jesus, on reaching the father's home, gives the kind reassurance that "the girl is not dead but just sleeping."[93]

The remarkable extent to which Matthew has completed the argument, only inadequately presented by the Sayings Gospel Q, that Jesus is the "one to come" can be shown visually in the following table. Across from each item in Q's list is given the Matthean location where that item has already taken place before the delegation from John arrives.[94]

Q's List	Matthew's Documentation
"the blind regain their sight"	Matthew 9:27–31, from Mark 10:46–52
"the lame walk around"	Matthew 9:1–8, from Mark 2:1–12
"the skin-diseased are cleansed"	Matthew 8:1–4, from Mark 1:40–45
"and the deaf hear"	Matthew 9:32–34, from Q 11:14
"the dead are raised"	Matthew 9:18–26, from Mark 5:22–43
"and the poor are evangelized"	Matthew 5–7, from Q 6:20–49

This documentation, showing that it is Jesus who does such acts of God, may in large part be due to an important contrast Matthew makes precisely in this regard between Jesus and John. Matthew edits the Q section about John and Jesus by inserting at its beginning and end the point that the issue is Jesus' *deeds*. At the beginning we hear:

Now when John heard in prison about the *deeds* of the Christ, he sent word by his disciples [95]

And at the end:

Yet wisdom is vindicated by her *deeds*. [96]

A significant parallel occurs in the Gospel of John. Jesus repeatedly points to his *deeds*, [97] which the Gospel of John then sets in contrast to the practice of John the Baptist:

And he went away again across the Jordan to the place where John was baptizing at first, and remained there. And many came to him and said: "John indeed *did no sign*, but as much as John said about this person was true." And many believed on him there. [98]

This contrast may also be the basis of the repeated comparison between John's and Jesus' ability to impart the Spirit—John did not have it, whereas Jesus did [99]—for it would be such "gifts of the Spirit" that would produce the deeds to document that contrast.

Jesus' superiority to John is driven home in the Sayings Gospel Q. Indeed, John is finally excluded from the Christian fold:

The least significant in God's kingdom is more than he. [100]

And John is the most obvious target when everyone except Jesus is bluntly declassified from knowing God; quite discreetly, though, John is not mentioned by name:

> Everything has been entrusted to me by my Father, and no one knows the Son except the Father, nor does anyone know the Father except the Son, and to whomever the Son chooses to reveal him.[101]

The concerted effort in the first third of the Sayings Gospel Q to prove Jesus to be the "one to come" whom John promised, an argument carried forward much more thoroughly in the first third of Matthew, would seem to have been a last-ditch appeal to that part of Judaism that would have been most open to following Jesus: the Baptists. Not only had Jesus begun as a Baptist, but both movements were similar in giving access to God directly. Neither of them said people had to appeal to the usual trappings of Jewish religion, such as the Jerusalem temple administered by the Sadducees, the local "clergy" of Pharisees and exegetes of the Law, and the Jewish festivals and rituals. All such things were part of a lifestyle that John and Jesus had no doubt practiced most of their lives, but that had now lost its decisive significance. So the disciples of Jesus had every reason to seek conversions among Baptists as the broader mission to Judaism in general had less and less success.

But the results of a mission among Baptists seem also to have been meager, though perhaps a step in this direction is preserved in Matthew. Already Mark had narrated the legend of the beheading of John by Herod Antipas at the instigation of his wife Herodias.[102] Matthew retells this story[103] with the significant addition of a reference to John's disciples at the conclusion:

His disciples . . . went and told Jesus. Now when Jesus heard this, he withdrew from there in a boat *to a lonely place apart.*[104]

What is surprising in this Matthean addition to Mark about John's disciples is that much of the wording of the addition also comes from Mark, but from a different story. It is Mark's conclusion to the mission of Jesus' own twelve apostles.

The apostles returned to Jesus, and told him all that they had done and taught. And he said to them, "*Come apart to a lonely place,* and *rest* a while."[105]

Other parts of this language had already been used once by Matthew—at the conclusion of Jesus' speech to those who had gone out in the wilderness to see John.[106] There Jesus invites them:

Come to me, all who labor and are heavy laden, and I will give you *rest.*[107]

This passage functions in Matthew as the conclusion to his expanded and improved demonstration that Jesus is the "one to come."[108]

All in all, Matthew seems to have in a sense fused in his mind the return of Jesus' own apostles from the preaching mission on which he had sent them and the return of John's disciples to Jesus on the death of John. The Sayings Gospel Q merely reports that, after Jesus supplies John's delegation with the list of his achievements proving him to be the "one to come,"[109] Jesus warns them:

Blessed is whoever is not offended by me.[110]

Thereupon they just disappear without a trace:

> And when they had left . . .[111]

Matthew may have reasoned as follows: He had already added, at the opening of Q's narration of John's sending a delegation to Jesus, the detail that John was in prison.[112] He may well have imagined that John's disciples reported back to him in prison, but then, after the beheading of John, came to Jesus to become his disciples. It remains unclear to what extent this may have actually happened or was just Matthew's wishful thinking. Perhaps both! In any case, all this may serve as a corrective to our normal assumption that John's and Jesus' followers were two distinct Jewish groups. It may be more accurate to think of them as for a time two overlapping parts of the same movement.

In all this, Matthew seems to be trying to do justice to Q's effort to win over the Baptists, the most accessible segment of Judaism, before giving up and copying rather slavishly the contents of Mark for the rest of his Gospel in order to commend himself to the gentile Christian church.[113] The last resort of Jesus' followers does seem to have been to turn to the Gentiles. This step had been taken rather readily by Paul, but the Galilean disciples of Jesus himself, represented by the Q community that became the Matthean community, seemed to have held out as long as they could, for they thought they could quote Jesus on their side:

> Do not go away on a road of the Gentiles, and enter no town of the Samaritans, but go rather to the lost sheep of the house of Israel. . . . When they persecute you in one town, flee to the next; for truly I tell you, you will not have gone through all the towns of Israel before the son of man comes.[114]

But then the Gospel of Matthew ends with the "great commission" of the resurrected Jesus, canceling the restriction on evangelizing Gentiles and instead calling on followers to "make disciples of all nations," though quite intentionally including the Sayings Gospel Q in their mission:

> . . . teaching them to obey everything that I have commanded you.[115]

WHEN DID IT ALL REALLY BEGIN?

We are inclined to think Christianity began either at Christmas or at Easter. But the earliest view of when it all began may have been with John the Baptist! Indeed, this may have been Jesus' own view:

> The Law and the Prophets were until John. From then on the kingdom of God is violated and the violent plunder it.[116]

But for Jesus' disciples, beginning with John came to mean less John's own ministry and death than it did Jesus' baptism by John, for it was then that he received the Spirit from God, marking for them the sharp difference between Jesus and John.

The Sayings Gospel Q and the canonical Gospels of Mark and John all begin their narrations with John the Baptist. It was only a later view that Jesus' story should, more like a biography, begin with his birth. So Matthew and Luke began their Gospels, though based on Q and Mark, with infancy narratives absent from Q and Mark.[117] But Luke was so committed to the idea that the story must begin with John that he began his Gospel with the birth narrative of John in his first chapter and then followed it with the birth narrative of Jesus in his second chapter.

Luke carries his emphasis on beginning with John throughout the book of Acts. When the question arises as to who should succeed Judas Iscariot as the twelfth apostle, Luke (in Acts) makes clear:

> So one of the men who have accompanied us during all the time that the Lord Jesus went in and out among us, beginning from the baptism of John until the day when he was taken up from us—one of these must become a witness with us to his resurrection.[118]

Luke used this definition for Matthias, the apostle to replace Judas, presumably because it was the current definition of the other eleven apostles, though it may well not have been actually the case. Luke in his own Gospel does not report that the twelve were with Jesus at the time he was baptized by John. Only Andrew is actually said to have been a Baptist.[119]

The role of John as marking the beginning is carried throughout Acts. Luke reports in Peter's sermon to Cornelius at Caesarea:

> That message spread throughout Judea, beginning in Galilee after the baptism that John announced . . .[120]

Then when Luke presents Paul preaching in the synagogue of Antioch in Pisidia, he has him sketch the history of Israel down to Jesus, whom he introduces by saying:

> Before his coming John had already proclaimed a baptism of repentance to all the people of Israel.[121]

Luke is clearly convinced that it all began with John's baptism.

THE CONTINUATION OF THE BAPTISTS

Yet it is Luke who concedes the ongoing existence of the Baptists as a somewhat distinct, only half Christian subgroup, in references to them continuing for some time.[122] After Paul had founded the church in Ephesus, an Alexandrian Jew named Apollos showed up in the synagogue:

> He had been instructed in the Way of the Lord; and he spoke with burning enthusiasm and taught accurately the things concerning Jesus, though he knew only the baptism of John.[123]

Aquila and Priscilla take him in hand and instruct him further, whereupon he is sent to Corinth as an evangelist. But then when Paul returns to Ephesus, he finds a dozen others who were baptized only into John's baptism. He has them rebaptized and lays his hands on them, with the desired Christian result:

> The Holy Spirit came upon them, and they spoke in tongues and prophesied.[124]

Thus there was apparently an ongoing Baptist movement that was not yet fully Christianized, but that Jesus' followers cultivated. Indeed, there is still today a baptizing sect in Iraq and Iran called the Mandeans (which in their language means "gnostics") who claim to go back to John, which could well be the case.

SIX

———•◆•———

JESUS' LIFESTYLE UNDERWRITTEN BY GOD HIMSELF

The best the narrative Gospels could do by way of presenting Jesus' Galilean ministry was to assemble disparate anecdotes. So they portray Jesus just wandering from place to place doing good until, halfway through the narrative, they have him leave Galilee to go to Jerusalem to die as the real purpose of his being on earth. But is it not more reasonable to assume that Jesus did in fact have something in mind for his Galilean ministry? We can get at it by looking at his lifestyle.

THE MISSION INSTRUCTIONS

The best indication we have of Jesus' actual lifestyle in Galilee is found in the "mission instructions" he is portrayed as giving to his disciples when he sent them out to evangelize the Jewish villages. The fact that there are two separate accounts, one in Q and one in Mark, each quite similar to the other, indicates that they both go back to a very archaic description they shared. This then gives a very clear impression of what Jesus' own lifestyle must have been, for it was basic to all Jesus had to say that one should practice what one preaches:

> Why do you call me: "Master, Master," and do not do what I say? Everyone hearing my sayings and acting on them is like a person who built one's house on bedrock; and the rain poured down and the flash floods came, and the winds blew and pounded that house, and it did not collapse, for it was founded on bedrock. And everyone who hears my sayings and does not act on them is like a person who built one's house on the sand; and the rain poured down and the flash floods came, and the winds blew and battered that house, and promptly it collapsed, and the fall was devastating.[1]

It is reasonable to assume that Jesus himself listened to what he had to say and acted accordingly. If he had not walked the walk as well as talked the talk, his disciples would surely not have reported that he said it.

Of course we should not assume that on a given day Jesus stood up in front of the apostles and literally gave the mission instructions as a speech. Rather, they are a description of the actual practice of the Jesus movement as it was still being carried out by the community that recorded the mission instructions. But its practice must have been based on what Jesus himself over time instructed it to do, indeed himself had exemplified.

With the passage of time, the mission instructions would have needed "updating." As practice changed or problems arose, the instructions would have changed to provide whatever clarification had become necessary. This is particularly obvious in the case of the Gospel of Matthew. The Matthean church grew out of the Q movement and so reflected the ongoing mission practice of that movement. Then Matthew merged the updated mission in-structions of the Sayings Gospel Q[2] with the mission instructions he found in the narrative Gospel Mark,[3] as well as much other material, to produce a greatly enlarged update of the mission in-structions.[4]

Initially, the disciples had gone from door to door asking for bed and breakfast without knowing at all what reception they would receive. Sometimes they would be admitted, sometimes not:

Into whatever house you enter, first say: "Peace to this house!" And if a son of peace be there, let your peace come upon him; but if not, let your peace return upon you. . . . Into whatever town you enter and they do not take you in, on going out from that town, shake off the dust from your feet.[5]

Of course, over time, certain houses would have become known as a soft touch, "safe houses." So by the time of the Gospel of Matthew, the instructions sound less like one is going at it cold and more as if one is looking up a house known for its hospitality on the basis of previous experience:

Whatever town or village you enter, find out who in it is worthy, and stay there until you leave.[6]

A clear instance of the narrative Gospel Matthew updating the Sayings Gospel Q in the light of ongoing experience has to do with the injunction that disciples were not to have a job on the side, since their work in Jesus' mission made them unpaid "work-ers" for the cause. Such "workers" were to live off of the hospital-ity of those who took them in. This had originally come to expression in the formulation:

For the worker is worthy of one's *reward.*[7]

But this saying came to be abused and interpreted to mean that the worker could ask for *money.*

This became a common abuse. (It is not unknown even today!) Indeed, it is explicitly cited and repudiated in the *Didache,* an archaic manual of church order that, though it did not get into the New Testament, is almost as old as the Gospels that did (see Chapter 10):

> Now concerning the apostles and prophets, deal with them as follows, in accordance with the rule of the gospel: Let every apostle who comes to you be welcomed as if he were the Lord. But he is not to stay for more than one day, unless there is need, in which case he may stay another. But if he stays three days, he is a false prophet. And when the apostle leaves, he is to take nothing except bread until he finds his next night's lodging. But if he asks for *money,* he is a false prophet.[8]

Now this abuse of taking money seems to have raised its ugly head already in the Matthean church, for the language has been altered just enough to avoid what sounded like permission, by changing "reward" to "food":

For the worker is worthy of one's *food.*[9]

Lest the point be missed, the Gospel of Matthew adds:

You received without payment, give without payment.[10]

Matthew also makes the same point in another way. The original injunction to "carry no purse"[11] has been made more explicit:

Take no gold, or silver, or copper in your belts.[12]

These constant clarifications in the mission instructions in Matthew are largely absent from the parallel text in Luke, for Q's mission instructions are actually no longer being followed in Luke's gentile church as it moves about in the big wide world beyond Galilee. Because Luke's gentile Christian church had long since gone over to the practice exemplified by Paul in the book of Acts, it would have been less involved in updating the archaic mission instructions of the Jewish Christians found in the Sayings Gospel Q. As a result, Luke remained closer to the original language of Q's mission instructions—thank goodness!

The Gospel of Luke in fact includes two separate sets of mission instructions, one from the Gospel more directed at Gentiles, Mark,[13] and one from the Gospel more directed at Jews, Q.[14] Luke's own mission policy becomes clear in considering the way Luke presents Paul's missionary journeys in the book of Acts. Actually, Paul himself had made his own divergent policy quite clear:

> Am I not free? Am I not an apostle? Have I not seen Jesus our Lord? Are you not my work in the Lord? If I am not an apostle to others, at least I am to you; for you are the seal of my apostleship in the Lord. This is my defense to those who would examine me. Do we not have the right to our food and drink? Do we not have the right to be accompanied by a believing wife, as do the other apostles and the brothers of the Lord and Cephas? Or is it only Barnabas and I who have no right to refrain from working for a living? . . . If others share this rightful claim on you, do not we still more? Nevertheless, we have not made use of this right, but we endure anything rather than put an obstacle in the way of the gospel of Christ.[15]

Paul's policy, out there in the vast gentile world of the Roman Empire, was of necessity different from Jesus' policy in the small Jewish villages of Galilee. After all, Paul did not hitch a ride on a sailboat to cross the Sea of Galilee, but must have bought a ticket (or its equivalent) on a ship to cross the Mediterranean (except when he was a guest of the Roman army!).[16] He even made a point of collecting money rather than going without a penny in his pocket, since he carried the collection back with him to Jerusalem for "the poor" there.[17] And he may well have carried baggage, namely, whatever equipment he needed to practice his profession as a tentmaker.[18]

It is thus surprising that the Gospel of Luke even went to the trouble and embarrassment of presenting Q's Jewish mission instructions at all.[19] Apparently Luke was treating them more as a museum piece displaying how things had been done at the heroic beginnings. Recall that, in the opening of Acts, Luke also presents the idealized beginnings of the church: there was a kind of communal kitty into which all the funds of those in the church were assembled, to be used for the needs of all.[20] Barnabas was the shining example:

> He sold a field that belonged to him, then brought the money, and laid it at the apostles' feet.[21]

But this policy was no longer being observed in the remainder of the book of Acts, no doubt partly because abuses showed it to be impractical; Ananias and his wife Sapphira were the case study:

> But a man named Ananias, with the consent of his wife Sapphira, sold a piece of property; with his wife's knowledge, he kept back some of the proceeds, and brought only a part and laid it at the apostles' feet.[22]

They died as a result of their deceit.

Just as Luke reported ancient rules no longer in practice, Matthew inserted no-longer-valid sayings opposing a gentile mission into his mission instructions,[23] even though by Matthew's time they had been largely canceled out. Matthew reports Jesus giving, in a resurrection appearance, the "great commission" to carry on a gentile mission.[24]

As a result of such archaizing tendencies on his part, Luke's version of Q's mission instructions is nearer to the Sayings Gospel Q, and hence to Jesus himself, than are the mission instructions of the other Gospels. It is precisely because the Lukan church itself did not follow the mission instructions, and so did not need to update them, that we can more easily reconstruct the original Q text from Luke:

> Carry no purse, nor knapsack, nor sandals, nor stick, and greet no one on the road. Into whatever house you enter, first say: "Peace to this house!" And if a son of peace be there, let your peace come upon him; but if not, let your peace return upon you. And at that house remain, eating and drinking whatever they provide, for the worker is worthy of one's reward. Do not move around from house to house. And whatever town you enter and they take you in, eat what is set before you. And cure the sick there, and say to them: "God's reign has reached unto you." But into whatever town you enter and they do not take you in, on going out from that town, shake off the dust from your feet. I tell you: For Sodom it shall be more bearable on that day than for that town.[25]

Luke not only copies these mission instructions of the Sayings Gospel Q much as they stand; he proceeds to cancel them out, as

no longer applicable, as soon as he finishes copying the whole of
the Sayings Gospel Q.[26] At this juncture Luke reports the following scene of Jesus with his apostles:

> He said to them, "When I sent you out without a purse,
> bag, or sandals, did you lack anything?" They said, "No, not
> a thing." He said to them, "But now, the one who has a
> purse must take it, and likewise a bag. And the one who has
> no sword must sell his cloak and buy one. For I tell you, this
> scripture must be fulfilled in me, 'And he was counted
> among the lawless'; and indeed what is written about me is
> being fulfilled." They said, "Lord, look, here are two
> swords." He replied, "It is enough."[27]

In this way Luke has shown respect for the outdated mission instructions—after all, the disciples had lacked nothing when following them! But he now proceeds to replace them in order,
quite literally, to arm his disciples in preparation for the following
Markan story of the arrest:

> But one of those who stood near drew his sword, and struck
> the slave of the high priest, cutting off his ear.[28]

But at this juncture we can turn away from the church militant
envisaged by Mark and return to Q's much more pacifistic mission instructions, which provide our clearest impression of Jesus'
own lifestyle during his Galilean ministry.

JESUS' GALILEAN MINISTRY

We should not underestimate the extent to which Jesus felt called
upon to assume a completely new lifestyle after having been so
immersed in John's message as to undergo his initiation. Jesus

must have believed that, in spite of appearances, the givens of life were basically changed: as the ideal becomes real and God rules,[29] there are to be no poor[30] or hungry,[31] no handicapped or sick,[32] no exploiter[33] or enemy,[34] no mentally disturbed[35] or force of evil.[36] Jesus believed that this ideal was the basic reality and acted accordingly.[37] But how do you do that in daily life?

Luke portrays John as answering some such practical questions for those who asked,[38] but not himself engaging in a new lifestyle back in everyday society. He maintained his role as baptizer at the Jordan River and thus in a sense avoided the problem for himself.

In the rite of passage administered by John, Jesus may have taken off all his identifying garb as an intentional repudiation of his past identity and then resumed, perhaps only out of modesty, the basic shirt and cloak of his day.[39] But he may not have resumed wearing sandals.[40] The absence of sandals would have involved such hardship in that very rocky terrain that many have hesitated to think it is meant to be taken literally. But it must have been meant literally, just as everything else in the mission instructions seems to be describing actual practice. Indeed, it is presupposed when John is described as not being worthy to take off Jesus' sandals;[41] this is a metaphor for not being worthy to baptize him, from which we can infer that people were immersed barefooted. Barefootedness is a standard symbol of penance (for example, among Franciscan monks) and may well have been characteristic of those baptized by John.

Jesus carried no coin purse,[42] for he had no coins and earned no money. Nor did he wear a knapsack,[43] for he took with him no change of clothes or provisions of food. What you should not do is store up funds in a purse or food and clothing in a knapsack, as if you may have lucked out with God today, but tomorrow you never know what will happen, so you have to be prepared for the worst! No, tomorrow, start out just as you started out today, praying:

Let your reign come: Our day's bread give us today.[44]

You should trust that God will reign each day just as he reigns today.

Jesus carried no stick,[45] the weapon of the poor, but remained defenseless. The injunction not to carry a stick is clearly intended to prevent self-defense against humans and even wild animals. The term hardly refers to a walking cane ("stave" in the King James translation; "staff" in the New Revised Standard Version; "stick" in the New English Bible). Rather, it means a club, the poor man's weapon. This is presupposed in the injunctions not to defend oneself against attack, but to turn the other cheek, give the shirt off one's back, go the second mile, and let oneself be exploited to the hilt:

> The one who slaps you on the cheek, offer him the other as well; and to the person wanting to take you to court and get your shirt, turn over to him the coat as well. And the one who conscripts you for one mile, go with him a second. To the one who asks of you, give; and from the one who borrows, do not ask back what is yours.[46]

Jesus counted on life's necessities being provided without his working[47] or otherwise concerning himself for his own physical well-being,[48] at least if we assume he practiced what he preached. This new life involved moving away from home and family ties, in Jesus' case from Nazareth to Capernaum.[49]

You may well wonder how Jesus, much less anyone else he might have talked into it, could have sustained a life of such radical deprivation. He may indeed have chosen a site for his Galilean ministry where such literal rigors as barefootedness, giving the shirt off one's back, taking no provisions for the trip, and having no form of self-defense were not utterly impossible.

The Sea of Galilee may have seemed best suited to the way of life he had in mind. It had the lowest altitude in Galilee, some 700 feet below sea level. So it would have had a milder winter climate than did the hill country Jesus came from, except perhaps when there was a storm at sea.[50] When the fishermen came to shore each dawn with their night's catch,[51] they would have been an easy touch for the local "holy man."[52] All this may have rendered the rigorous lifestyle Jesus practiced at least possible.

Jesus developed on the north shore a small circuit of three villages, Capernaum, Bethsaida, and Chorazin. These towns may also have been helpful. His base camp at Capernaum was still in Galilee, ruled by Herod Antipas, who had put John to death. But it was a border town, and Jesus befriended the Roman centurion stationed nearby.[53] It was on the frontier of the territory of Philip, a less threatening ruler. Bethsaida, across the frontier just outside Galilee, was in fact the capital of Philip's territory, so it may well have been politically safer. It was also the hometown of one of John's converts who became Jesus' first disciple, Andrew.[54] Perhaps it functioned as a Baptist haven of refuge, which would have welcomed Jesus, himself in effect a Baptist.

Such Baptist converts would, like Jesus himself, have been seeking to find their new way, and so would have been open to whatever guidance Jesus might have been able to offer. So Andrew joined Jesus, along with his brother Simon, whom Jesus called Peter. They, along with Philip, also from Bethsaida, are the first disciples listed in the Gospel of John.[55]

The Gospel of Mark lists Simon and Andrew, both fishermen, as the first converts,[56] and then two other fishermen, James and John:

> Immediately he called them; and they left their father Zebedee in the boat with the hired men, and followed him.[57]

Peter and Andrew, though from Bethsaida, had a home in Capernaum, which Jesus visited early on to heal Peter's mother-in-law of a fever.[58] This may well have become Jesus' base camp, for he is referred to when in Capernaum as being "at home."[59]

When Jesus' embarrassed family came to take him back home, since they thought he was making a fool of himself,[60] he repudiated them, declaring his disciples to be his true family.[61] He argued that one must "hate" family ties,[62] insisting that he had come to "divide" the generations in the home.[63] Indeed, he called on people to follow him and turn their backs on their home and families (as had he).

> He said to his disciples: "The harvest is plentiful, but the workers are few. So ask the Lord of the harvest to dispatch workers into his harvest."[64]

He would not accept a disciple who was not willing to make this sacrifice of family obligations:

> But another said to him: "Master, permit me first to go and bury my father." But he said to him: "Follow me, and leave the dead to bury their own dead."[65]

No matter how noble and selfless the motivation, the outcome of any success in enlisting followers would inevitably have been a disruption of home life.

The security provided by family and familiar village life would be more than compensated for because God would actually be functioning as a caring Father. This is where trust in the kingdom of God, God actually reigning, would come into play[66]—it's God's problem! It was this trust in a caring God that made you as carefree as the ravens and lilies.

Consider the ravens: They neither sow nor reap nor gather into barns, and yet God feeds them. Are you not better than the birds? . . . Observe the lilies, how they grow: They do not work nor do they spin. Yet I tell you: Not even Solomon in all his glory was arrayed like one of these. . . . So do not be anxious, saying: "What are we to eat?" Or: "What are we to drink?" Or: "What are we to wear?". . . For your Father knows that you need them all. But seek his kingdom, and all these shall be granted to you.[67]

This in turn is what explains the radical mission instructions, and thus what Jesus himself actually did during his Galilean ministry:

Carry no purse, nor knapsack, nor sandals, nor stick, and greet no one on the road.[68]

This was not an instance of the asceticism that was commonly part and parcel of the religious lifestyle of "holy men" of that day. Jesus' lifestyle was not ascetic, as is made clear by the caricature of him as a carouser compared to the ascetic John:

For John came, neither eating nor drinking, and you say: "He has a demon!" The son of humanity came, eating and drinking, and you say: "Look! A person who is a glutton and drunkard, a chum of tax collectors and sinners!"[69]

Indeed, the mission instructions go on to urge Jesus' followers, the "workers," to eat what is set before them in the house of the "son of peace" who takes them in:

And at that house remain, eating and drinking whatever they provide, for the worker is worthy of one's reward. Do not move around from house to house. And whatever town you enter and they take you in, eat what is set before you.[70]

It is just here that we catch sight of Jesus' explanation that was intended to make sense of all this unusual conduct, for the mission instructions go on:

And cure the sick there, and say to them: God's reign has reached unto you.[71]

The bestowal of "Peace" on the house, with the opening Jewish greeting "*Shalom,*"[72] and then this explanation of God having reigned among them provide Jesus' explanation of what has taken place in the household. Not only is the cure of the sick, like the exorcisms elsewhere,[73] ascribed to God reigning, but the provision of food is also God's kingdom coming, in the concrete sense of answering the petition of the Lord's Prayer:

Let your reign come: Our day's bread give us today.[74]

You do not go hunting for food and drink, any more than do the ravens.[75] You seek instead God's reign,[76] for you know that food and drink will be granted in the home of some "son of peace," where God's reign will happen as the answer to the Lord's Prayer.

——•◆•——

SEVEN

JESUS' TRUST IN GOD

It may come as a surprise to you that Jesus' trust in God derived primarily from his experience of nature. So this calls for some explanation.

NATURAL CALAMITIES AS ACTS OF GOD

In antiquity, the forces of nature were thought of as activated by God. It was God who caused the flood,[1] but in rainstorms he presents the rainbow as a promise he will not do it again.[2] It is God who brings "fire and brimstone" down on the wicked.[3] "Brimstone" is highly flammable sulfur and may refer to a natural disaster in an oil-rich terrain:

> On the wicked he will rain coals of fire and sulfur; a scorching wind shall be the portion of their cup.[4]

In the showdown between the priests of Baal and Elijah on Mt. Carmel as to whose god was really God, it was agreed:

> The god who answers by fire is indeed God.[5]

After Elijah had prayed to Yahweh:

> Then the fire of Yahweh fell and consumed the burnt offer-
> ing, the wood, the stones, and the dust, and even licked up
> the water that was in the trench. When all the people saw it,
> they fell on their faces and said, "Yahweh indeed is God;
> Yahweh indeed is God."[6]

For us today, it is difficult to imagine such an explanation of the
weather. When we hear the weather predictions on the news, we
are more likely to give the meteorologist credit or blame than
we are to think of God. But the older tradition does emerge at
times, when, for example, a drought leads a farming community
to come together at church to pray for rain. And in archaic legal
language, disasters of nature are still called "acts of God."

John the Baptist seems to have continued this view of disasters
as the acts of God in nature, but Jesus took quite the opposite
turn. He found his revelation of a caring, loving God in his observation of nature.

GOD'S CARING CONTROL OF NATURE

For Jesus, as for the rest of those in antiquity, it was quite natural
to think of God as responsible for nature. But Jesus had his own
quite distinct perception of what God was doing around him. Instead of a judgmental God wreaking vengeance on evil, he saw
everywhere the finger of a caring Father:

> Are not five sparrows sold for two cents? And yet not one
> of them will fall to earth without your Father's consent. But
> even the hairs of your head all are numbered. Do not be
> afraid, you are worth more than many sparrows.[7]

More familiar is his appeal to ravens and lilies to illustrate trust in that caring Father:

> Therefore I tell you, do not be anxious about your life, what you are to eat, nor about your body, with what you are to clothe yourself. Is not life more than food, and the body than clothing? Consider the ravens: They neither sow nor reap nor gather into barns, and yet God feeds them. Are you not better than the birds? And who of you by being anxious is able to add to one's stature a cubit? And why are you anxious about clothing? Observe the lilies, how they grow: They do not work nor do they spin. Yet I tell you: Not even Solomon in all his glory was arrayed like one of these. But if in the field the grass, there today and tomorrow thrown into the oven, God clothes thus, will he not much more clothe you, persons of petty faith! So do not be anxious, saying: "What are we to eat?" Or: "What are we to drink?" Or: "What are we to wear?" For all these the Gentiles seek; for your Father knows that you need them all. But seek his kingdom, and all these shall be granted to you.[8]

An even older form of this appeal to nature occurs in the *Gospel of Thomas*. It is in a very fragmentary copy of the Greek text dating back to the third century, whereas the reading we are familiar with about the lilies, "how they grow," is first attested in manuscripts of the fourth century. The very archaic text reads:

> [Jesus says: Do not be anxious] from dawn to [late, nor] from eve [to] dawn, either [about] your [food], what [you are to] eat, [or] about [your] robe, with what you [are to] clothe yourself. [You are] far better than the lilies, which do not card nor spin. [And] having one clothing, [. . .] you [. . .]?

Who might add to your stature? That one will [give] you
your clothing!⁹

Here the reading "do not card" rather than "grow" is apparently
the original text. The familiar text of the New Testament, and
hence of Q, points out here that lilies "grow." But in the context
this does not make a lot of sense. One would expect an illustration of how lilies trust God by not working, like the ravens, which
"neither sow nor reap nor gather into barns." Yet in Greek "not
card" is spelled very similarly to "grow" and fits right in place.

Back then, carding was part of the process of making clothes
in the home. Today we no longer have to take wool sheared from
sheep through several steps to get fabric from which to make
our own clothes. So the verb "card" may no longer even be in
your vocabulary (it has nothing to do with playing cards). Carding refers to aligning the wool fibers once they have been
cleaned. They are straightened and put mostly parallel, so the
wool can later be spun into yarn and woven into cloth. Jesus obviously knew a lot more about farm life back then than most of
us do today!

Lilies, which "do not card nor spin," are a role model for trusting God for one's needs. So this is apparently the original reading
in this saying, in which a scribal error very early on had changed
"not card" to "grow."

What is perhaps the most telling instance of Jesus' observation
of nature is his striking inference from the fact that the weather is
the same on both sides of the tracks (or, as would fit conditions
of that day somewhat better, on both sides of the trail):

Love your enemies and pray for those persecuting you, so
that you may become sons of your Father, for he raises his
sun on bad and good and rains on the just and unjust. The
one who slaps you on the cheek, offer him the other as well;

and to the person wanting to take you to court and get your shirt, turn over to him the coat as well. And the one who conscripts you for one mile, go with him a second. To the one who asks of you, give; and from the one who borrows, do not ask back what is yours.[10]

Presumably, in Nazareth the climate on the wrong side of the tracks (or trail) was always the same as the climate on the right side. What was unusual was for someone, Jesus, to draw such a radical ethic from this simple observation of nature. Here Jesus broke through the cultural conditioning that is in control of all of us and actually *saw God*—at work in nature around him. So when Matthew reports this part of the Q Sermon, he begins by pointing out the contrast:

You have heard that it was said, "You shall love your neighbor and hate your enemies." But I say to you, "Love your enemies and pray for those persecuting you . . . "[11]

For Jesus, God is in charge of nature, and on all sides is showing how he is—and how his children should be—kind to all, to the bad as well as to the good.

THE LAWS OF NATURE VERSUS MIRACLES

We, consciously or unconsciously, distinguish God's action from what can be understood as the laws of nature. The world rolls on its natural course, thanks to the laws of nature to which everything conforms. At the human level, we know we live our everyday lives under the laws of nature. So what does not conform to such laws we call "miracles." Jesus did not live in a world "schooled" by the laws of nature, as we do. So he did not perceive the problem we see as the "miraculous."

People can float naturally on top of the water in the Dead Sea, because the high salt content makes an equal volume of the water a bit heavier than a human body. But this is not true in the fresh-water of the Sea of Galilee. Matthew reports that Peter had to learn this the hard way.[12] So for Jesus to walk on the water of the Sea of Galilee is a "miracle."[13]

The milk of human kindness can quite naturally move people to share what little food they have with those even less fortunate. But to feed "five thousand men, besides women and children" from only "five loaves and two fish," with "twelve baskets full" left over, would have to be a "miracle."[14]

Jesus did not experience the world of nature as we do, separating what can be explained scientifically from what has to be miraculous. For him, the whole realm of nature was in God's hand, under God's control.

Sometimes God acted in more dramatic ways, which were referred to as "mighty acts" of God, "wonders" (literally, "powers") that stood out, such as exorcisms and healings:

> Woe to you, Chorazin! Woe to you, Bethsaida! For if the wonders performed in you had taken place in Tyre and Sidon, they would have repented long ago, in sackcloth and ashes.[15]

But to limit trust in God to such exceptional manifestations of his activity in nature leads to reproach:

> Unless you see signs and wonders you will not believe.[16]

Furthermore, in the world of the first century, such superhuman events could be ascribed to evil forces as well as to God:

> But some said: "By Beelzebul, the ruler of demons, he casts out demons!"[17]

"Beel-zebul," meaning "lord of dung," was a ridiculing corruption of "Baal-zebub," the god of the Philistines of Ekron.[18]

Again:

False Messiahs and false prophets will appear and produce signs and omens, to lead astray, if possible, the elect.[19]

But in the modern world we tend to think of it quite differently. What is hard to believe is precisely the miraculous! We even have disparaging terminology for the kind of faith that believes in miracles, such as "credulity," "gullibility," "superstition." Many people do indeed find the miracle stories to be the major problem in coming to grips with Jesus' trust in God.

But, as a matter of fact, the larger problem may lie in the other direction—seeing the natural as an act of God! Because of our distinction between laws of nature, on the one hand, and miracles of God, on the other, we tend to lose sight of the fact that Jesus considered all of the natural processes as under God's control, unified as acts of God. The one great exception was unnatural illness with weird symptoms caused by demon possession, against which God fought.[20]

Our problem is not so much what Jesus thought God was doing, such as "miracles," though they may well be things we do not think happen at all. Our more important problem is that the bulk of what Jesus thought God was doing are things that we do think happened—it is just that we do not recognize them as acts of God, since they are not miracles. We have, in effect, secularized the world of nature. Or, put otherwise, we have made ourselves into functional atheists, no matter whether we think we believe in God or not (see the Epilogue).

THE KINGDOM OF GOD TAKING PLACE

Jesus talked a lot about what God was doing. But he was a layperson, without theological education, and so did not use the jargon of the trade. Actually, the only real theological term that he constantly used was a rare expression, usually translated "kingdom of God," but perhaps better translated "God's reign," "God reigning." So it calls for some explanation.

Some people get confused by the fact that in the Gospel of Matthew the "kingdom of God" is usually referred to as the "kingdom of heaven," leading them to think that the kingdom is in heaven—something one can experience only in the afterlife or at the end of time. But Jesus was talking about God reigning in the here and now.

Use of the idiom "kingdom of heaven" is due to the fact that Matthew is the Gospel most closely related to Judaism and so still reflects its sensitivities. Jews have been so committed to not taking God's name in vain, which, after all, is one of the Ten Commandments,[21] that they have thought it best not to "take" God's name at all. That is, they do not pronounce Yahweh out loud at all. Sometimes they carry this so far that they not only avoid pronouncing Yahweh; they even avoid pronouncing "God" and instead simply refer to the "name," by which everyone in the Jewish community knows what they mean—God!

A striking instance of this Jewish reverence for God's personal name is found in the Dead Sea Scrolls. There are a few fragmentary Greek translations of the Hebrew scriptures among the scrolls. These Greek translations hesitate to change God's holy name from Hebrew into Greek, and so leave the Hebrew letters *HWHY,* which spell his name, in the middle of the Greek text. But these letters for God's name were not written in the form that Hebrew was written at that time, for the shape of the Hebrew letters themselves had by then evolved by adopting the Aramaic shape of the letters. The archaic original Hebrew shape of the letters had fallen completely out of use, except for this striking example: God's name should not only not be translated from Hebrew into Greek, but should not be written in Aramaic script, only in the original Hebrew script!

This reverence for God's name is no doubt the explanation for the opening of the Lord's Prayer. This prayer, apparently going back to Jesus himself, does not say God's name at all, but simply refers to God as "Father." In fact, the standard Jewish sensitivity about pronouncing God's name comes to expression in a somewhat parenthetical phrase:

—may your name be kept holy!—[22]

Even the prodigal son knew enough about his religion to avoid saying God's name out loud. So when he returned remorsefully to his father, he confessed:

Father, I sinned against heaven [!] and before you.[23]

The god of the Jews does have his own personal name, just as did the gods of the Canaanites, Baal and Ashtoreth; the gods of the Greeks, Zeus and Aphrodite; the Romans, Jupiter and Minerva; the Egyptians, Isis and Osiris; the Roman soldiers, Mithra; and so on. But the name of the Jewish god does not occur in translations of the Bible, since in the Middle Ages the rabbis intentionally flagged it as not to be pronounced when reading aloud.

In the written text of the Hebrew scriptures, God's name is of course present, probably to be pronounced Yahweh. But when the rabbis read out loud, out of reverence they substituted *Adonai,* meaning "Lord," each time they saw the word "Yahweh." And to make sure that no one would pronounce "Yahweh," they inserted the vowels for "Adonai" beneath the consonants of "Yahweh" as a hint in the written text about how to read it out loud without taking God's name in vain.

Some Christians, reading the Hebrew scriptures as handed down by the rabbis, did not understand that this vowel-consonant arrangement meant to substitute "Adonai" for "Yahweh" when reading the text. So they tried to pronounce the consonants of the Hebrew word "Yahweh" with the vowels of the Hebrew word "Adonai" and came up with a nonexistent name for God, Jehovah. Actually, "Jehovah" did get into translations of the Bible, once as early as William Tyndale's translation of 1530,[24] but frequently in the Revised Version of the nineteenth century. But now that the misunderstanding has been recognized, it is of course no longer used (except by Jehovah's Witnesses).

There were of course many ways in which Jewish custom avoided pronouncing God's true name. The instance with which we are most familiar is Matthew's "kingdom of heaven." But since the other Gospels and Paul use "kingdom of God," we assume that Jesus himself used that term, although this is hardly more than an assumption. This idiom, "kingdom of God" (or "kingdom of heaven"), is Jesus' favorite term for talking about God acting in our own world, whether God's action is what we would call a "miracle" or not.

Jesus must have realized that God is not always fully reigning now, since so much evil still prevails. Up to this point one may speak of Jesus' "eschatology"—a doctrine of "last things"—and leave it at that. But the kingdom of God was not for Jesus just a cosmic revolution such as John the Baptist had talked about so excitedly. (If it had been, its imminent expectation would have been invalidated by the passage of time; indeed, the whole idea would have been rendered unintelligible for us by the Enlightenment.) But for Jesus, acts of God reigning were real in his world of experience, and it is that reality on which we need to focus our attention.

I begin with the best-known text in the Sayings Gospel Q, the Lord's Prayer. Matthew has glossed the prayer several times to enrich it according to the more liturgical usage of his own congregation. One of these Matthean additions is the petition:

Thy will be done on earth as it is in heaven.[25]

Apparently this petition was not in Jesus' own prayer. It is not that Jesus would have had anything against this idea. It is just that the Lukan form of the prayer is thought to be older, nearer the form of the prayer in Q, and so nearer to Jesus' own prayer. But in Luke this petition is absent.[26] Apparently the petitions originally ran as follows:

Let your reign come:
Our day's bread give us today;
and cancel our debts for us,
as we too have canceled for those in debt to us;
and do not put us to the test![27]

There is of course in the (King James) Bible also a familiar doxology at the end of the Lord's Prayer:

For thine is the kingdom, and the power, and the glory, for ever. Amen.[28]

This is a liturgical response that was usually recited or chanted when the Lord's Prayer was used in church, and so gradually crept into manuscripts of the Gospel of Matthew, and thus into the King James translation. It was still absent from the oldest and most reliable manuscripts.

The Lord's Prayer is clearly not a prayer about the afterlife or another world, but about the here and now. Indeed, the interpretation of the Lord's Prayer, which follows directly in the Sayings Gospel Q, makes this abundantly clear:

> Ask and it will be given to you, search and you will find, knock and it will be opened to you. For everyone who asks receives, and the one who searches finds, and to the one who knocks will it be opened. What person of you, whose child asks for bread, will give him a stone? Or again when he asks for a fish, will give him a snake? So if you, though evil, know how to give good gifts to your children, by how much more will the Father from heaven give good things to those who ask him![29]

This hardly means that as surely as a human parent gives bread and fish in the here and now, the heavenly Father will give "pie in the sky by-and-by." It clearly means that God will answer the petition "Our day's bread give us today" in the here and now, daily.

Perhaps this present reality of God reigning is made most clear in the case of exorcism:

> But if it is by the finger of God that I cast out demons, then there has come upon you God's reign.[30]

The abnormal symptoms of a disease that led it to be called possession by a demon or an evil spirit are in the here and now:

> "Teacher, I brought you my son, for he has a spirit that makes him unable to speak; and wherever it seizes him, it dashes him down; and he foams and grinds his teeth and becomes rigid."

> And they brought the boy to him; and when the spirit saw

him, immediately it convulsed the boy, and he fell on the ground and rolled about, foaming at the mouth.

"It has often cast him into the fire and into the water, to destroy him."[31]

Of necessity the exorcism, as the coming of God's reign, is also in the here and now:

And after crying out and convulsing him terribly, it came out, and the boy was like a corpse; so that most of them said, "He is dead." But Jesus took him by the hand and lifted him up, and he arose.[32]

The extent to which a day's bread and exorcisms are already God reigning is made clear in the mission instructions:

And whatever town you enter and they take you in, eat what is set before you. And cure the sick there, and say to them: "God's reign has reached unto you."[33]

As a result of God reigning in the here and now, the people of the Q community thought they were already "in" the kingdom:

There has not arisen among women's offspring anyone who surpasses John. Yet the least significant in God's kingdom is more than he.[34]

A woe pronounced against exegetes of the Law, who shut people out of the kingdom, does not just refer to closing access to the kingdom in the afterlife, when one might otherwise have hoped to enter it. Rather, it refers to these exegetes of the Law as themselves not having entered the kingdom, as well as having excluded others, already now:

> . . . for you shut the kingdom of God from people; you did not go in, nor let in those trying to get in.[35]

Another woe gives an illustration of what may be meant by not letting people in:

> And woe to you, exegetes of the Law, for you bind burdens, and load on the backs of people, but you yourselves do not want to lift your finger to move them.[36]

Another saying pinpoints rather precisely a point in time when the kingdom is in history, namely, just after the Law and the Prophets and John, for it is after then that the kingdom is violated and plundered:

> The Law and the Prophets were until John. From then on the kingdom of God is violated and the violent plunder it.[37]

It is difficult to understand why the kingdom of God is seen not only as present, but also as undergoing violence since John—unless the death of John is itself taken to be the beginning of the violent process that was continuing in the case of the Jesus movement, for the suppression of the movement did continue in violent ways. The saying may even presuppose the death of Jesus.

The parables of the mustard seed[38] and the yeast[39] present the kingdom of God as having begun already and still continuing to develop. The transition from seed to tree and from yeast to dough, both of which we consider natural processes, were for antiquity processes carried out by God. These parables do not limit the kingdom to the future, but describe it as something thrown now into the garden, hid now in three measures of flour. God is reigning already now.

To be sure, God's reign is not intended as a "given" status, like the "established church," as if God reigning had been turned over by God to a sometimes all too human hierarchy to run. Rather, God reigning is something that actually happens from time to time as God participates in the living experience of people.

Jesus rejected the idea of specifying any given place where the kingdom can be expected to come at some time in the future, since in fact it is already present in the here and now:

> But on being asked when the kingdom of God is coming, he answered them and said: "The kingdom of God is not com·ing visibly. Nor will one say: 'Look, here!' Or: 'There!' For look, the kingdom of God is within you!"[40]

Again, this saying should not be misunderstood, as if it had in view just a mystic inwardness. Though the rare preposition translated here "within" does seem to mean inside in contrast to outside, the meaning would not seem to be far from the other alternate translations "among you" and "in your midst," since it does mean "within" society, standing over against some never-never land "out there." The point of the saying is that the kingdom is not something that will take place somewhere sometime, but is a reality in the present experience of people in the world today. So Jesus could call on people to "seek" the kingdom:

> But seek his kingdom, and all these shall be granted to you.[41]

This is anything but hunting for some future cosmic event, which Jesus had explicitly rejected. Rather, this seeking is set over against the other kind of seeking, which anxiety-ridden Gentiles do when they ask:

"What are we to eat?" Or: "What are we to drink?" Or: "What are we to wear?"[42]

Hence, "seeking" the kingdom returns full circle to the petition "Let your reign come" in the Lord's Prayer. People do not need to be anxiety-ridden about scrounging for such physical necessities as food to eat, for they can trust in God reigning, that is, answering the petition for God's reign to come in the concrete form of providing one day's bread.

Thus the kingdom of God, the one clearly recognizable "technical term" in Jesus' vocabulary, in a sense elevates to religious relevance much of everyday living, such as sickness, the need for food and clothing, and the evil with which people are always struggling. It is in the real, everyday world that God reigning is very good news, Jesus' gospel.[43]

It is no coincidence that the oldest collection of Jesus' sayings, what we call the Sermon (what Matthew expanded into the Sermon on the Mount), begins by pronouncing just such down-and-outers fortunate: it is the poor, the hungry, the mourners who are "blessed."[44] The kingdom of God is not God's stamp of approval on the status quo, the powers that be, the ruling class. Rather, it is countercultural, for it gives hope to the hopeless. It is not consoling them with "pie in the sky by-and-by," but involves concrete intervention in the lives of the needy, mitigating their plight in the here and now.

IT CUTS BOTH WAYS

Jesus' message about God reigning was of course a call to his listeners to put their trust in God's being there when they need him. This means in practice counting on God to work through other people on our behalf. The petition "Our day's bread give us today" is not intended to be answered by bread falling from heaven, but rather by a "son of peace" who provides bed and breakfast:

> And at that house remain, eating and drinking whatever they provide, for the worker is worthy of one's reward. Do not move around from house to house. And whatever town you enter and they take you in, eat what is set before you.[45]

But this cuts both ways. God reigning is equally a call to take an active role in meeting the needs of others:

> And cure the sick there, and say to them: "God's reign has reached unto you."[46]

There is an explicit reciprocity in what Jesus has to say about God reigning: we receive from God through what he motivates other people to do for us, and other people receive from God through what he motivates us to do for them.

This give and take comes to expression already in the Lord's Prayer:

> Cancel our debts for us, as we too have canceled for those in debt to us.[47]

Here it is quite clear that there is a reciprocal relationship between the answer to the prayer for forgiveness, on the one hand, and the forgiving action of the one praying for forgiveness, on the other.

Although the language about "canceling debt" did function idiomatically to refer to forgiving sin, it seems also to have been meant literally with regard to forgiving financial debt:

> To the one who asks of you, give; and from the one who
> borrows, do not ask back what is yours.[48]

Individuals whose debt has been canceled by God intervening on
their behalf with a creditor, and who are thus put back on their
feet with a chance to function normally in society, can in turn be
expected to forgive the debts of those who owe them money.

People are not comfortable with their religion becoming this
down-to-earth. But one of Jesus' parables insists on precisely this
point:

> The kingdom of heaven may be compared to a king who
> wished to settle accounts with his slaves. When he began
> the reckoning, one who owed him ten thousand talents was
> brought to him; and, as he could not pay, his lord ordered
> him to be sold, together with his wife and children and all
> his possessions, and payment to be made. So the slave fell
> on his knees before him, saying, "Have patience with me,
> and I will pay you everything." And out of pity for him, the
> lord of that slave released him and forgave him the debt.
> But that same slave, as he went out, came upon one of his
> fellow slaves who owed him a hundred denarii, and seizing
> him by the throat, he said, "Pay what you owe." Then the
> fellow slave fell down and pleaded with him, "Have patience
> with me, and I will pay you." But he refused; then he went
> and threw him into prison until he would pay the debt.
> When his fellow slaves saw what had happened, they were
> greatly distressed, and they went and reported to their lord
> all that had taken place. Then his lord summoned him and
> said to him, "You wicked slave! I forgave you all that debt
> because you pleaded with me. Should you not have had
> mercy on your fellow slave, as I had mercy on you?" And in

anger his lord handed him over to be tortured until he would pay his entire debt. So my heavenly Father will also do to everyone of you, if you do not forgive your brother or sister from your heart.[49]

This responding to others just as you trust God will respond to you is in practice very different from the kind of give and take that is usual in society. The king forgave a large debt owed him, but did not expect the slave in return to forgive the king. No quid pro quo was involved at all. The king expected, and got, nothing in return for his kindness. Rather, the slave was expected in turn to be forgiving toward the debt of his own fellow slave. The king punished his slave not for failing to reciprocate to him, but rather for failing to reciprocate to someone else.

Thus the reciprocal relation is not between the forgiving person and the forgiven person, but between the forgiven person and another person in need of forgiveness. The person who is forgiven is of course ultimately indebted to God, who motivated the other to do the forgiving. But God then calls upon the forgiven person to reciprocate by forgiving some third person, and so it proceeds, as God reigns from one to the next.

The "normal" kind of reciprocity, with which we are all quite familiar, is motivated by self-interest and so is rejected by Jesus:

If you love those loving you, what reward do you have? Do not even tax collectors do the same? And if you lend to those from whom you hope to receive, what reward do you have? Do not even the Gentiles do the same?[50]

Of course Jesus' call to forgive debts with no gift in return also applies to forgiving in general. Just as we pray daily for God's forgiveness, just so we are to forgive daily:

> If your brother sins against you, rebuke him; and if he repents, forgive him. And if seven times a day he sins against you, also seven times shall you forgive him.[51]

This way of conceiving of God (and hence ourselves) as constantly forgiving may recall the shockingly flippant and presumptuous witticism of the French Enlightenment: "Forgiving? That's what God is there for. It's just his job!" It is not surprising that Jesus' shocking view of God as the constant forgiver has been largely ignored—as has, all too often, the corollary that forgiving is what we too are there for—it's our job too! That is, you are to respond to others just as you trust God will respond to you:

> Be full of pity, just as your Father is full of pity. Do not pass judgment, so you are not judged. For with what judgment you pass judgment, you will be judged. And with the measurement you use to measure out, it will be measured out to you.[52]

The reciprocity among equals in human relations is also familiar from the "Golden Rule," present in most cultures throughout the world, and ascribed to Jesus as well:

> And the way you want people to treat you, that is how you treat them.[53]

But this too can be reduced to an age-old principle of self-interest. In the Roman Empire it was called the patronage system and was even codified in the Latin expression *Do ut des*, "I give so that you give"; in the animal world, it is "I scratch your back so you scratch mine." In modern politics, it is called euphemistically "special interests." Lobbyists get elected officials to vote for the legislation that favors the firms whose "generous" campaign gifts made it pos-

sible for the officials to get elected in the first place. This is how
elections are "bought": our firm treated you well in your last election campaign, so you treat our firm well in the way you vote, and
our firm will treat you equally well in your next election campaign.

But for Jesus, the reciprocity is between us and God, not between us and others. We are to forgive another person because
God has forgiven us—irrespective of how the other person acts
toward us! Self-serving favoritism does not deserve the term
"love," for love shows itself to be real by being directed toward
persons who have nothing they can do for us by way of return. So
Jesus called for love to go far beyond one's kinsfolk, neighbors,
peer group, patron, and campaign contributors. As a result, his
new love commandment is much less known, not to speak of
being much less practiced:

> Love your enemies and pray for those persecuting you, so
> that you may become sons of your Father, for he raises his
> sun on bad and good and rains on the just and unjust.[54]

It is for this reason that Matthew contrasts Jesus' unique call to
"love your enemies" with that age-old policy of blood vengeance:

> You have heard that it was said, "You shall love your neigh-
> bor and hate your enemy."[55]

This ugly, back side of love of neighbor is why blood feuds
never end.

Blood feuds have plagued society for millennia and are still
common in some parts of the world. I have experienced them between villages next to each other in Upper Egypt. The discoverer
of the Nag Hammadi Codices, Muhammad Ali, told me that
someone from the opposing village had murdered his father,
whereupon his mother told him and his brothers to keep their

mattocks sharp. Their chance came six months later, when someone told them that the murderer was asleep by the side of the
road nearby. They rushed out and hacked him to pieces, dividing
his heart among them to eat, the ultimate act of blood vengeance.

All this was told me in response to my asking Muhammad Ali
to show me where he discovered the jar with the codices inside.
Understandably enough, he was not willing to show me the site
of the discovery, since it was near the opposing village. So I went
to the opposing village, found the son of the murdered murderer,
and asked him if he would take vengeance on Muhammad Ali if
he had the chance. He replied by telling me the story of his
avenging his father's death. He took a group of young men and
sneaked up on a funeral procession of Muhammad Ali's clan—
they shot them up, killing a dozen. So he considered the issue set-
tled and would not need to kill Muhammad Ali to even the score.

I brought this good news back to Muhammad Ali, reassuring
him that he could show me the site of the discovery without en-
dangering his own life. He opened his shirt, showed me a scar just
above his heart, and replied that they had wounded him in the
shoot-out of the funeral procession, but had not killed him. But if
he could get his hands on the man who tried to kill him, he would
kill him on the spot. So this sort of feud can go on, back and
forth, forever.

Jesus' call on us to love our enemies not only calls a halt to
blood feuds of such a literal kind, but goes beyond what has always been considered justice ever since Hammurabi's code: an
eye for an eye, a tooth for a tooth. This was not meant cruelly, but
as fairness, preventing the powerful from taking undue retalia-
tion. Rather than overkill, let the punishment fit the crime! (Still
today in Saudi Arabia the punishment for a robber is not death,
but just cutting off the offending hand!) In our own society, punishment is also supposed to be "fair," though of course in less
bloody terms (except for capital punishment).

The point is, you cannot build a society larger than your own group if love does not go beyond your neighbor. It is that narrow, noninclusive view of society that is transcended by the command to love your enemy. The kingdom of God is an inclusive society, for God loves everybody—and so should you.

If the Golden Rule and love of neighbor call on us to return good for good, Jesus' "love your enemies" calls on us to return good for bad, to turn the other cheek, to go the second mile, to give the shirt off our back—literally, for Jesus is where these expressions come from:

> The one who slaps you on the cheek, offer him the other as well; and to the person wanting to take you to court and get your shirt, turn over to him the coat as well. And the one who conscripts you for one mile, go with him a second. To the one who asks of you, give; and from the one who borrows, do not ask back what is yours.⁵⁶

The only way to make sense of this is to realize that you yourself are on the receiving end of such love of enemies. Jesus' perception of nature comes into play, in which he finds God to be revealed in the sun rising on evil persons and the rain showering the fields of the unjust. In situations in which you yourself have been evil or unjust and yet received through God's intervention so much more than you deserve, you can only be grateful for this second chance. But the second chance is a chance to reciprocate, now to do good to your enemies and pray for your persecutors. Those who hear this and act accordingly are what Jesus called "sons of God," persons in whose conduct "God reigns." Such men and women are what we today might call the "true church," for it is this that might change an evil society into the kingdom of God. That is why it became Jesus' gospel.

EIGHT

———◆———

JESUS' VIEW OF HIMSELF

Jesus did not apply titles to himself, which makes it difficult for people to come to grips with who he thought he was. The key to who he thought he was, however, does not lie in titles, but in what he said and did. This little book about what he said and did is designed to give you a clearer impression of who he was than any list of titles ascribed to him could ever do. As a matter of fact, titles can be very misleading, since they come with associations from their own past, which they tend to superimpose on the picture of Jesus. But what he said and did is the bedrock information on which any attempt to understand what he was up to, what his gospel is, has to be based.

THE ABSENCE OF DISTINCTIVE TITLES OF JESUS

We may well find it difficult to cope with the idea that Jesus used no titles for himself, for titles are a built-in part of the picture of Jesus with which we are familiar. In fact, in our society the title "Christ" has become for all practical purposes Jesus' "last name," even to the extent that "*Jee*-sus *Christ!*" has become a slang term meaning no more than "Gosh!" or "Wow!"

The title "Christ" is Greek for "Messiah," which is Hebrew for "the anointed person." The idea goes back to when the king of Israel was "anointed" by God's prophet to that office as a kind of inauguration ceremony. But once Israel, from the Babylonian captivity on, had no king, the title referred to the hoped-for future king who would reign when Israel would once again be a sovereign nation. But such a king seemed never to emerge—until Christians identified Jesus as that king to come and so called Jesus "Messiah," in Greek "Jesus Christ."

The Sayings Gospel Q never uses the title "Christ." Since Q is the largest collection of sayings of Jesus, many of which do go back to him, it is clear that he did not use the title of himself. Nor is there reference in Q to the main Old Testament prophecy attached to that messianic hope:

> But you, O Bethlehem of Ephrathah, who are one of the little clans of Judah, from you shall come forth for me one who is to rule in Israel, whose origin is from of old, from ancient days.[1]

Bethlehem is named in the prophecy, because it was the hometown of the king who founded the Israelite dynasty, David.[2] Clearly, to report that Jesus was born in Nazareth would not have fit the title of Christ nearly so well. Instead, Mary and Joseph have to be brought to the right place in time for Christmas in Bethlehem.[3]

This in turn was associated with another prophecy:

> Look, the young woman is with child and shall bear a son, and shall call him Immanuel.[4]

The "young woman" of the Hebrew text becomes "virgin" in the Greek translation used by Christians.

It is these two prophecies that are brought together by Matthew as fulfilled by Jesus. Actually, the birth narratives of Matthew[5] and Luke[6] diverge from each. Otherwise the narratives diverge from each other in almost all details, except for the names of the parents, Mary and Joseph, and of course the name of the baby. But none of all this is in the Sayings Gospel Q, in conformity with the absence there of the title "Christ."

SONS OF GOD

Perhaps the loftiest sounding title used of Jesus in the Gospels is "Son of God." At his baptism, a voice from heaven calls out:

You are my Son, the Beloved; with you I am well pleased.[7]

This was of course the Gospels' way of elevating Jesus above John in the baptism scene. But it posed a potential danger from the Christian point of view. It might give the impression that it was only then that Jesus became God's Son! This possibility was strengthened in some manuscripts of Luke, which used the language of a psalm to suggest God adopted Jesus at his baptism:

You are my son; today I have begotten you.[8]

This notion ended up as the heresy of adoptionism, which maintained that Jesus became God's Son only when God adopted him at his baptism.

Matthew and Luke forestall such an outcome by prefacing the baptism story with their infancy narratives, according to which God engendered Jesus already at his conception. Matthew reports:

But before they lived together, she was found to be with child from the Holy Spirit.⁹

Luke explains that an angel told Mary:

The Holy Spirit will come upon you, and the power of the Most High will overshadow you; therefore the child to be born will be holy; he will be called Son of God.¹⁰

The Gospel of John forestalled the same problem by identifying Jesus with God from the very beginning of it all:

In the beginning was the Word, and the Word was with God, and the Word was God.¹¹

Apparently the Sayings Gospel Q also reported Jesus' baptism, including the heavenly voice designating him as Son, for this is presupposed in Q's temptation narrative, where the devil exploits this title to tempt Jesus to assume a pompous role for himself:

If you are God's Son, order that these stones become loaves.

If you are God's Son, throw yourself down.¹²

The final temptation for Jesus was the offer to make him a prestigious ruler, since that is what the title "Son of God" implied in the ancient world. In the Roman Empire the title was used of rulers, such as the emperor, or legendary heroes, such as Hercules:

And the devil took him along to a very high mountain and showed him all the kingdoms of the world and their splendor, and told him: "All these I will give you, if you bow down before me.""[13]

The Sayings Gospel Q presents Jesus as resisting all such temptations latent in the title "Son of God." But then Q, in its subsequent effort to win over vacillating persons such as the disciples of John, does present Jesus as his Father's unique Son by asserting that he alone provides access to God.

Everything has been entrusted to me by my Father, and no one knows the Son except the Father, nor does anyone know the Father except the Son, and to whomever the Son chooses to reveal him.[14]

Jesus was anything but the pompous hero associated with the title "Son of God" in the Roman Empire. But once that title was superimposed on him, it became inevitable for him to be portrayed in a way that became increasingly imperial, domineering, and threatening.

Once the Roman Empire became Christian, calling Jesus "Son of God" functioned in that wrong way. The power of the Christian emperor of the Byzantine Empire rested on his claim to be the delegate on earth of that foreboding Son of God. It is this grimly frowning, overbearing face of the Son of God that stares down from a golden mosaic on the ceiling in the cupola of the magnificent Byzantine cathedral Hagia Sophia in Istanbul, Turkey, the ancient Byzantine capital Constantinople. There it once cowed the local population into obeying absolutely Christ's emissary, the Byzantine emperor.

This title, when used of Jesus in this way, could pervert him into the very opposite of what he was. And this is all the more ironic, indeed tragic, since he seems to have used the title "son of

God" in the very reverse meaning, and not just of himself, but also of his followers. He exhorted them:

> Love your enemies and pray for those persecuting you, so that you may become sons of your Father, for he raises his sun on bad and good and rains on the just and unjust.[15]

This saying would not of course have been welcomed by kings, who wanted to guarantee a subservient, fearful population. So it may be no coincidence that the King James Bible obscured this identification of simple people who love their enemies with the true sons of God. It translated the middle clause: "that you may be *children* of your Father." The noun translated "children" is the same noun used in the title "Son of God," but the association is safely hidden by this translation, which was no doubt chosen since it was "politically correct" for its day.

It was Jesus' simple disciples in Galilee who were sons—and of course daughters—of God. Whenever Jesus called upon them to think of God as their Father,[16] he was by implication calling upon them to think of themselves as his sons and daughters.

THE SON OF HUMANITY

The most common designation for Jesus, the term characteristic of his own usage, is "son of man." This is often mistaken as a messianic title, though it was not used that way in rabbinic Judaism. It is not a title at all, but rather a Semitic idiom meaning simply an instance of the "human" race. Similarly, the idiom "daughters of Jerusalem" is not a title, but simply a way of referring to women from Jerusalem, Jerusalemites.[17] Another instance of this kind of Semitic idiom occurs when Jesus refers to the head of a household who, in response to his greeting "Peace," admits Jesus or his disciple for bed and breakfast. Jesus calls him a "son of peace," that is, a peaceful person.[18]

Similarly "son of man" really means no more than son of humanity, an instance of the human race, a human being. Hence, it is just a synonym for "human," as in the parallel lines of a psalm.[19] The King James translation is word for word:

> What is man, that thou art mindful of him?
> and the son of man, that thou visitest him?

The freer, but accurate, modern translation of the New Revised Standard Version reads:

> What are human beings that you are mindful of them,
> mortals that you care for them?

Here the self-effacing self-designation "son of man" is accurately rendered simply "mortals."

This idiom meaning "human" is an unassuming way to refer to oneself as early as the book of Ezekiel, in which each of Ezekiel's visions begins when God addresses him as "son of man," meaning only "son of humanity," "you human," "frail mortal that you are."[20] We have already pointed out, in the case of the founder of the Dead Sea sect, the "Teacher of Righteousness," that a shortage of adjectives made prepositional phrases play the role of adjectives—"Teacher of Righteousness" really just means "Righteous Teacher." In the same way "son of man" really just means "human person."

This idiom for "human" has been misunderstood as if it were primarily an apocalyptic title based on one occurrence in the book of Daniel.[21] Daniel is narrating a vision spanning the world history of his day in which a series of beastly empires (lion, bear, leopard, and a fourth unnamed beast representing Rome) would be followed by a worldwide kingdom ruled on God's behalf by a son of man, that is, by a son of humanity, a human, rather than by a beast. The point is that it will be a humane kingdom.[22] The book of Daniel is not giving the ruler a title, but distinguishing the humane Jews from the beastly Romans.

Some modern translations do simply say "human," rather than the cumbersome and misleading "son of man." But to bring to expression the simple meaning a "human" while retaining the flavor of the Semitic idiom, I use the formulation "son of humanity" in my translation of the Sayings Gospel Q and also in what follows.

This idiom is used once in the *Gospel of Thomas:*

> Foxes have their holes and birds have their nest. But the son of humanity has no place to lay his head down and to rest.[23]

Here, as in Daniel, the idiom is used to contrast with the animal world the homelessness of the human sphere, since all animals have some kind of home. This same saying occurs in the Sayings Gospel Q[24] in the context of Jesus warning off all too casual applicants for discipleship, one of whom wanted to continue living at his family home until his father had passed away.[25] The saying makes the point that one must "count the cost" before joining a homeless wandering band of Jesus' disciples.

Especially in the Sayings Gospel Q, Jesus often uses the same self-effacing idiom of himself:

> Whoever says a word against the son of humanity, it will be forgiven him; but whoever speaks against the holy Spirit, it will not be forgiven him.[26]

It is used by opponents who deride him:

The son of humanity came, eating and drinking, and you say: Look! A person who is a glutton and drunkard, a chum of tax collectors and sinners![27]

A blessing is pronounced on Jesus' disciples who, as a result of following him, are derided and persecuted:

Blessed are you when they insult and persecute you, and say every kind of evil against you because of the son of humanity.[28]

Conversely, the idiom is used of Jesus as a prophet warning of impending judgment:

For as Jonah became to the Ninevites a sign, so also will the son of humanity be to this generation.[29]

Jesus saw himself rising up on the day of judgment as a character witness:

Anyone who may speak out for me in public, the son of humanity will also speak out for him before the angels. But whoever may deny me in public will be denied before the angels.[30]

In the last saying "son of humanity" is not a messianic title referring to Jesus as judge at the last judgment (a concept all too familiar to us from the Apostles' Creed). Actually, it seems that in this saying it is angels who are envisaged as the judges. Jesus, like the queen of the South (the queen of Sheba, who came to pay homage to Solomon[31]) and the Ninevite men (who repented at the preaching of Jonah[32]), is envisaged as a character witness testifying against those who have ignored his message:

> The queen of the South will be raised at the judgment with
> this generation and condemn it, for she came from the ends
> of the earth to listen to the wisdom of Solomon, and look,
> something more than Solomon is here! Ninevite men will
> arise at the judgment with this generation and condemn it,
> for they repented at the announcement of Jonah, and look,
> something more than Jonah is here![33]

Of course Jesus' role as character witness is not to be taken
lightly. He is the decisive character witness; that is, in substance
he determines one's fate. Whoever is, technically speaking, the
judge has no choice but to follow Jesus' recommendation! So
Jesus is in effect the judge. But it is interesting to note that he is
not yet accorded the title "Judge." As is the case with other titles
of Jesus that we take as givens, the Sayings Gospel Q shows them
only in the process of emerging.

It is unclear whether Jesus is meant as the judge in other instances, where the title "Judge" is not present, but Jesus may well
be conceived of as performing that function. This is the case with
a warning against being unprepared when Jesus comes, where
"Son of Humanity" does seem to function as a title and so is cap-
italized:

> You also must be ready, for the Son of Humanity is coming
> at an hour you do not expect.[34]

The idiom is then used of Jesus coming "on his day" at the end of
time:

> As the lightning streaks out from Sunrise and flashes as far
> as Sunset, so will the Son of Humanity be on his day.

> As it took place in the days of Noah, so will it be in the day

of the Son of Humanity. For as in those days they were eating and drinking, marrying and giving in marriage, until the
day Noah entered the ark and the flood came and took
them all, so will it also be on the day the Son of Humanity is
revealed.[35]

But outside of the Sayings Gospel Q, this role of the Son of Humanity coming at the end of time is painted in increasingly glori-
ous colors reminiscent of Daniel. In Mark:

Then they will see "the Son of Humanity coming in clouds"
with great power and glory. Then he will send out the angels, and gather his elect from the four winds, from the ends
of the earth to the ends of heaven.[36]

Matthew embellishes this even further, saying:

The sign of the Son of Humanity will appear in heaven, . . .
and they will see "the Son of Humanity coming on the
clouds of heaven" with power and great glory.[37]

It is all accompanied by "a loud trumpet call."
Here Daniel's language about the coming of the humane empire seems to have begun coloring Matthew's presentation of the
day of judgment. Daniel had put it:

I saw one like a son of humanity coming with the clouds of
heaven. And he came to the Ancient One and was presented before him. To him was given dominion and glory
and kingship, that all peoples, nations, and languages should
serve him. His dominion is an everlasting dominion that
shall not pass away, and his kingship is one that shall never
be destroyed.[38]

Matthew introduces his presentation of the last judgment similarly:

> When the Son of Humanity comes in his glory, and all the angels with him, then he will sit on his glorious throne. Before him will be gathered all the nations . . .[39]

Here Jesus, the simple human, just one son of humanity, is assimilated to Daniel's picture of "one like a son of humanity coming with the clouds of heaven" to reign over the nations at the final judgment. But this is the final outcome of the development of Christian usage, not its point of departure with Jesus. The point of departure is the self-effacing sayings and action of Jesus, which claimed nothing for Jesus himself *except that God was speaking and acting in what he said and did.*

When you think about it, what higher claim could he possibly have made? After all, as a Jew he would have conceived of it as blasphemy to claim to be God. But this transition from God's decisive spokesperson to God himself is a development in the gentile church that is very understandable. Give him a title that fits his function! But it is we who gave him that title, not he himself.

JUDGES ON THE DAY OF JUDGMENT

"Judge" is indeed another concept for Jesus, familiar from the Apostles' Creed, where it is said that he will "come to judge the living and the dead." But it too does not actually occur in the Sayings Gospel Q, though it almost does.

As in the case of the title "sons of God" and the role of the son of humanity as a character witness on the day of judgment, Jesus judging at the last judgment is a role shared with others. He can, rather casually, point out that the children of those accusing him of being in cahoots with Beelzebul will judge the accusers in the last judgment. These children, like Jesus himself, are exorcists, and so know better:

> And if I by Beelzebul cast out demons, your sons, by whom do they cast them out? This is why they will be your judges.[40]

The claim is not that at the last judgment Jesus will be the judge of his accusers, but that their own sons will be the judges!

Similarly the Sayings Gospel Q concludes with Jesus assuring his followers that they will function as judges at the final judgment, which by implication should include Jesus, though this is not actually mentioned:

> You who have followed me will sit on thrones judging the twelve tribes of Israel.[41]

It is Matthew who elevates Jesus to the role of judge at the day of judgment. He takes this decisive step in his enlargement of the conclusion of the Sayings Gospel Q:

> In the new world, when the Son of Humanity shall sit on his glorious throne, you who have followed me will also sit on twelve thrones, judging the twelve tribes of Israel.[42]

SOPHIA'S CHILDREN

"Wisdom," in Greek "Sophia," meaning God's wisdom, was a personification for God, a way of talking about God's action in human circles while at the same time protecting the sublime transcendence of God above. Since in both Hebrew and Greek (as well as in Latin) "wisdom" is a feminine noun, this might supply the missing feminine dimension of God.

"Wisdom" is another term that the Sayings Gospel Q uses in association with Jesus to the extent that it almost becomes a title. The series of woes against the Pharisees and exegetes of the Law culminates in a final criticism ascribed to Sophia, Wisdom:

> Therefore also Wisdom said: I will send them prophets and sages, and some of them they will kill and persecute, so that a settling of accounts for the blood of all the prophets poured out from the founding of the world may be required of this generation, from the blood of Abel to the blood of Zechariah, murdered between the sacrificial altar and the House. Yes, I tell you: An accounting will be required of this generation!
>
> O Jerusalem, Jerusalem, who kills the prophets and stones those sent to her! How often I wanted to gather your children together, as a hen gathers her nestlings under her wings, and you were not willing! Look, your house is forsaken! I tell you: You will not see me until the time comes when you say: "Blessed is the one who comes in the name of the Lord!"[43]

Of course it is not Jesus who often went to Jerusalem to enlist the Jerusalemites in his cause, but rather Sophia who sent her prophets again and again to Jerusalem down through the centuries.

The idea of Jesus himself going frequently to Jerusalem to enlist disciples is found only in the Gospel of John. This is what accounts for the traditional assumption that Jesus' public ministry lasted three years, to provide time enough for him to attend all the annual Jewish festivals that the Gospel of John reports he attended. But today it is generally agreed that here, as often, it is the synoptic Gospels, Matthew, Mark, and Luke, that are correct in presenting Jesus going only once during his public ministry to

Jerusalem, where he was executed. So it is more correct to think of his public ministry as lasting only a year, or even less.

Luke tones down the reference to personified Wisdom as speaking herself by using the expression "the Wisdom *of God* said,"[44] and Matthew eliminates the expression completely, so as to make it simply another saying of Jesus: "Therefore I send you prophets . . ."[45]

Personified Wisdom recurs in a second place in the Sayings Gospel Q. The section about John and Jesus reaches its climax by pointing out that, in spite of the snide caricatures of both John and Jesus, they will win out in the end. But the way this is actually brought to expression is that it is Wisdom herself who is to be vindicated:

> For John came, neither eating nor drinking, and you say: "He has a demon!" The son of humanity came, eating and drinking, and you say: "Look! A person who is a glutton and drunkard, a chum of tax collectors and sinners!" But Wisdom was vindicated by her children.[46]

Here it is not the case that Jesus is actually given the title Sophia, for in any case the reference would have to be to John as well as Jesus. The "children" of Sophia are either John and Jesus, or their disciples, or both. And, since Sophia has been sending prophets as her delegates since the beginning of time, John and Jesus are just the culmination in a long series of such delegates from Abel to Zechariah and on down to the time of the Q community.

THE ONE TO COME

From this survey it is clear that most of the so-called christological titles of Jesus are not yet present in the Sayings Gospel Q, have not yet fully become such titles at the time of Q, or have not been narrowed down to refer to Jesus alone in Q. But there is still another dimension to Q's archaic nature in this regard. In Q two terms that were in the process of becoming titles have in effect fallen out of use in later Christianity. We have already seen this to be the case with "Sophia," which, apart from an occasional romantic poet, had to wait until the rise of modern feminism to come into its own as a divine title.

The second such designation occurs in John the Baptist's pointing forward to "one to come" to hold the day of judgment. John no doubt meant this to refer to God, but in the Sayings Gospel Q it is reinterpreted to refer to Jesus in the section about John's delegates coming to Jesus to ask:

> Are you the one to come, or are we to expect someone else?[47]

The answer of the Sayings Gospel Q is a resounding affirmation that Jesus is indeed the "one to come":

> Go report to John what you hear and see: The blind regain their sight and the lame walk around, the skin-diseased are cleansed and the deaf hear, and the dead are raised, and the poor are evangelized.[48]

We have seen that the Sayings Gospel Q provided some evidence to back up the claim that Jesus is the "one to come" prophesied in Isaiah, but that Luke, and even more so Matthew, had to add a great deal of material to make that claim more credible. But then this "title" seems to fade away.

In the Sayings Gospel Q, the idiom recurs with reference to Jesus coming at the day of judgment:

> I tell you: You will not see me until the time comes when

you say: "Blessed is the one who comes in the name of the Lord!"[49]

But here it is not a title, just the part of a psalm traditionally used of pilgrims going up to Jerusalem for the Passover festival:

Blessed is the one who comes in the name of the Lord![50]

The term recurs in all the canonical Gospels when Jesus is entering Jerusalem at the "triumphal entry," but here again it is not a title at all, just part of the traditional psalm:

Hosanna! Blessed is the one who comes in the name of the Lord![51]

Matthew, Luke, and John each make this acclaim more Christian by adding titles for Jesus that they had at their disposal:

Hosanna to the Son of David! Blessed is the one who comes in the name of the Lord! Hosanna in the highest heaven!

Blessed is the king who comes in the name of the Lord! Peace in heaven, and glory in the highest heaven!

Hosanna! Blessed is the one who comes in the name of the Lord—the King of Israel![52]

But each of these Gospels shows that the "one to come" has not really become a title for Jesus, precisely because the exaltation of Jesus has to be added to by means of the other titles.

All four canonical Gospels had already taken measures to shift the meaning of John the Baptist's reference to the "one to come" away from God to make it refer to Jesus. Yet they did not use it as a title, but reduced it to a mere time reference: Jesus came later than John. Mark changes the "one to come" into a verb form, so as to read:

The one who is more powerful than I is coming after me.[53]

Matthew makes another adjustment, so that the expression merely means "the one who is coming after me," identifying Jesus merely as a disciple of or successor to John:

The one who is coming after me is more powerful than I.[54]

The Gospel of John makes the same adjustment as does Matthew:

The one who is coming after me.[55]

And then Luke presents Paul, preaching in Ephesus to disciples of John, making this same adjustment:

John baptized with the baptism of repentance, telling the people to believe in the one who was to come after him, that is, in Jesus.[56]

If it were not that the issue is so prominent in Q, as to whether Jesus is really the prophesied "one to come," we would not know that this expression ever existed as a potential title for Jesus.

JESUS AS GOD'S SPOKESPERSON

We are accustomed (largely through the influence of the Gospel of John) to think of Jesus as claiming credit for what he was and did. After all, in the Gospel of John, Jesus says "I am" everything—"the bread of life," "the light of the world," "the gate," "the good shepherd," "the way, and the truth, and the life,"[57] and so on. But this way in which the Gospel of John showed reverence for Jesus can backfire today. Was he on a grandiose ego trip? Was he a narcissist?

Fortunately, this is not the way Jesus thought of himself. It may be hard for us, here as elsewhere, to get behind what is so familiar in this regard, but here again it is the Sayings Gospel Q that points the way. Perhaps the Sayings Gospel Q makes this clearest in the case of exorcism. When Jesus' exorcisms are ascribed by the crowds to his being in cahoots with "Beelzebul, the ruler of demons,"[58] Jesus' response is not to claim credit for himself as an exorcist, but rather to point to God doing it:

> But if it is by the finger of God that I cast out demons, then there has come upon you God's reign.[59]

It is not even claimed that only Jesus has this special access to God's finger. Rather, the same explanation is assumed for the success of other exorcists as well:

> But if I by Beelzebul cast out demons, your sons, by whom do they cast them out?[60]

The implied answer is that these other exorcists cast out demons by the same power as does Jesus—the power of God!

The reason one is to be free from anxiety like ravens and lilies, with regard to the basic necessities of life such as food and clothing, is also because of God:

> For your Father knows that you need them all.[61]

This is immediately explained by a more familiar equivalent to "God's finger," which we have run across again and again: "God's kingdom."

But seek his kingdom, and all these shall be granted to you.[62]

Jesus usually ascribes what he does to God doing it, for we have seen that the idiom traditionally translated the "kingdom of God" is perhaps better translated "God's reign," or, more actively still, "God reigning."

The mission instructions are presented as what Jesus told his disciples when he sent them out, but these instructions no doubt describe the lifestyle Jesus himself lived, as we have seen. If admitted by the head of the house, who thereby becomes a "son of peace," one is told what to do:

Eat what is set before you. And cure the sick there.[63]

But one is also instructed to explain this action:

And say to them: "God's reign—God reigning—has reached unto you."[64]

So here too it is God's active ruling, rather than Jesus' or his disciples' status or ability, that provides the explanation, for what happens is the answer to prayer:

Let your reign come: Our day's bread give us today.[65]

That is, Jesus does not understand himself as being any kind of personage in his own right; he "merely" does what God does through him. Here the Gospel of John does put it much the way Jesus himself would put it:

I do nothing on my own, but I speak these things as the Father instructed me.[66]

Jesus was not on some kind of ego trip, but felt under compulsion to say and do what he was convinced God wanted said and done. This is why his disciples could pick up where he left off.

JESUS' VIEW OF HIS OWN DEATH

Of course Jesus' Galilean disciples, even those who had not gone up to Jerusalem with him to Passover, knew of the tragic outcome of that pilgrimage and shared the shock of those who had witnessed the horrible scene. But the sensitivity in the Sayings Gospel Q that Jesus is part of a larger group—sons of God, prophets and sages as children of Wisdom/Sophia, and character witnesses and judges at the day of judgment—helps us understand the absence from the Sayings Gospel Q of a passion narrative confined only to his death to the exclusion of all others who have died for God's cause.

In Q, John and Jesus are of course understood as being the culmination of the list of Wisdom's prophetic delegates who have been consistently killed from the time of Abel on. Indeed, the lament over Jerusalem for killing the prophets sent to her down through the ages has at its climax a reference to Jesus:

> I tell you: You will not see me until the time comes when you say: "Blessed is the one who comes in the name of the Lord!"[67]

So the Sayings Gospel Q clearly presupposes Jesus' death as the culmination of the prophets sent by Wisdom and killed by the Jerusalemites, yet without isolating his death as the saving event par excellence, as the church is accustomed to think of it.

The exclusive role of Jesus' death is derived from Paul's exclusive focus on Jesus' crucifixion:

> For I decided to know nothing among you except Jesus
> Christ, and him crucified.[68]

The lengthy passion narratives of all four canonical Gospels have
a similar focus, though of course they also include what preceded
the Passion:

> For the son of humanity came not to be served but to serve,
> and to give his life a ransom for many.[69]

But in the Sayings Gospel Q the situation with regard to Jesus'
death is similar to the situation with regard to titles: Q has not
yet narrowed the field so as to focus only on Jesus, for Jesus himself apparently did not narrow the field to focus only on himself.
    Obviously Jesus knew of the beheading of John, but just how
he coped with that tragedy is hard to say. Perhaps one saying in Q
about John may give a suggestion:

> The Law and the Prophets were until John. From then on
> the kingdom of God is violated and the violent plunder it.[70]

But Jesus' predictions of his own death, which in Mark go into
such detail that they are clearly summaries of Mark's own passion
narrative, are no longer thought to go back to Jesus himself:

> The son of humanity must undergo great suffering, and be
> rejected by the elders, the chief priests, and the scribes, and
> be killed, and after three days rise again.

> The son of humanity is to be betrayed into human hands,
> and they will kill him, and three days after being killed, he
> will rise again.

See, we are going up to Jerusalem, and the son of humanity will be handed over to the chief priests and the scribes, and they will condemn him to death; then they will hand him over to the Gentiles; they will mock him, and spit upon him, and flog him, and kill him, and after three days he will rise again.[71]

But the recognition that Jesus did not make such pedantic and detailed predictions of his own death should not obscure the much more important point. By what he said and did, he was taking his own life into his hands, and he must have known it. He did not have a martyr complex, but he was selfless enough and committed so fully to his cause that he was prepared, come what may, to stay the course.

NINE

—•◆•—

THE END AS THE
BEGINNING

Jesus' living out of his own gospel all came to a horrible end on
"Good" Friday.

THE HORROR OF THE CRUCIFIXION

Mark ends the crucifixion story with Jesus' last cry:

"O my God! O my God! Why have you abandoned me?"[1]

This cry is too much for Luke, who simply omits it.

All one can say medically is that Jesus died gasping for breath,
the physical end point of crucifixion:

Then Jesus gave a loud cry, and breathed his last.[2]

Luke, instead, has Jesus die on a more edifying note:

"Father, into your hands I commend my spirit." Having said
this, he breathed his last.[3]

John too has a more fitting end:

"It is consummated!"[4]

Jesus' death seems to fly in the face of all he had said about trusting completely in God as a caring Father:

Your Father is full of pity.[5]

Again:

Are not five sparrows sold for two cents? And yet not one of them will fall to earth without your Father's consent. But even the hairs of your head are all numbered. Do not be afraid, you are worth more than many sparrows.[6]

Again:

What person of you, whose child asks for bread, will give him a stone? Or again when he asks for a fish, will give him a snake? So if you, though evil, know how to give good gifts to your children, by how much more will the Father from heaven give good things to those who ask him![7]

Again:

Do not be anxious about your life, what you are to eat, nor about your body, with what you are to clothe yourself. . . . If in the field the grass, there today and tomorrow thrown into the oven, God clothes thus, will he not much more clothe you, persons of petty faith! So do not be anxious, saying: "What are we to eat?" Or: "What are we to drink?" Or: "What are we to wear?". . . Your Father knows that you need them all. But seek his kingdom, and all these shall be granted to you.[8]

Yet on the cross, he says:

"I am thirsty!"[9]

Jesus died hungry—what was he to eat? Thirsty—what was he to drink? Naked—what was he to wear?

It must have been a simply terrible thing to witness, seeing a loved one hanging there in excruciating pain, hour after hour, with cold-blooded soldiers from the army of occupation casually standing guard lest you approach and try to help. The realization must have come crashing down upon the disciples, if they had any sense at all, that it had been a wonderful dream that had nothing to do with reality. They had no choice but to give up trying to "fish for people"[10] and return to Galilee to resume fishing for fish.[11]

THE REAL REALITY OF RESURRECTION FAITH

Yet Jesus' death was not the last word, for the Sayings Gospel Q belies that obvious assertion! It was only after Jesus' crucifixion that all his trusting words about a caring heavenly Father were repeated, collected, and recorded by his disciples, ultimately to reach us in Matthew and Luke in the New Testament. And this took place not as a nostalgic, sad memory of what they had so hoped might be true, but now knew was much too good to be true.

Quite the contrary: They began all over again to proclaim Jesus' message, as if nothing could happen, not even the worst, to shake their faith. Jesus' faith had survived the beheading of John, and the disciples' faith survived the crucifixion of Jesus, for they heard him still saying:

What I say to you in the dark, speak in the light; and what
you hear whispered in the ear, proclaim on the housetops.
And do not be afraid of those who kill the body, but cannot
kill the soul.[12]

What matters is integrity, not external circumstances or even life
span. They realized that what Jesus said is still true, even in the
most desperate of situations!

One by one, then in smaller or larger groups, the disciples experienced Jesus still calling on them to continue his message and
lifestyle. Thus he reentered their lives as they experienced anew
the reality of his message and in turn were commissioned to carry
it on just as he had. This is the experience that was and is the reality of Easter.

Paul records a tradition in which these early witnesses to the
resurrection are tabulated, to which he, somewhat sheepishly,
adds his own experience:

For I handed on to you as of first importance what I in turn
had received: that Christ died for our sins in accordance
with the scriptures, and that he was buried, and that he was
raised on the third day in accordance with the scriptures,
and that he appeared to Cephas, then to the twelve. Then
he appeared to more than five hundred brothers and sisters
at one time, most of whom are still alive, though some have
died. Then he appeared to James, then to all the apostles.
Last of all, as to one untimely born, he appeared also to me.[13]

It is perhaps relevant to notice that this oldest tradition, going
back to the disciples themselves, does not narrate the actual stories with which we are most familiar, such as Paul's blinding-light
experience on the Damascus road,[14] the appearance to Mary

Magdalene at the empty tomb,[15] the breaking of bread with disciples on the Emmaus road,[16] and the doubting Thomas story.[17]

But it is neither the empty tomb nor the appearances that created the Easter faith. It is, rather, the other way around. This may
come as a bit of a surprise, so let me try to illustrate it from our
modern experience of Christmas and Easter with our children.

We know how to tell them that the Christmas tree and Santa
Claus do not make Christmas, that it is the other way around:
Jesus' birthday makes them! If Jesus had not been born, we would
have no Christmas tree or Santa Claus. And the Easter rabbit and
Easter eggs do not make Easter, but the other way around: Jesus'
resurrection makes them! If Jesus had not been raised from the
dead, there would be no Easter rabbit or Easter eggs. So we can
not lose sight of Jesus' birth and resurrection, which is too easy to
do (and not only for children), flooded as we are with all the ad-
vertisements for what is on sale at such holidays.

Just as we tell our children that they must think behind the
trappings to the substance of Christmas and Easter, just so we
must as adults think more deeply. It is not the resurrection stories
that make Easter, but the other way around. It was his disciples
experiencing Jesus still making his point, as a gospel still real even
after his death, that created the Easter stories. So that is the only
valid form of Christian faith today. Easter faith is taking Jesus at
his word, that God is a heavenly Father who really cares, who
reigns for us and through us in our daily lives. Easter was not just
the launching of another religion of a dying and rising God, of
which the ancient world had already too many. It was the disciples' renewed experience of Jesus saying again that God continues to be there for us, and for others through us, in spite of the
horror of "Good" Friday. That is indeed good news, the gospel of
Jesus risen from the dead.

TEN

THE GOSPEL OF JESUS AND THE GOSPEL OF PAUL

Paul never had an opportunity to meet Jesus during Jesus' life-time, and later on he had only very limited contact with the disci-ples.[1] After all, his first contacts were in order to persecute them![2] But when those who had such personal ties with Jesus contrasted their close ties to Jesus with Paul's lack of familiarity with Jesus, he defended himself by playing down the importance of having known Jesus personally.[3] The church has tended to follow his lead until recently, when what we can know about Jesus himself has come to center stage.

PAUL ECHOES JESUS' SAYINGS

Paul did not seem called upon to quote sayings of Jesus to ac-credit himself. Indeed, his opponents in the church might have won at that game! They might even have been able to quote Jesus opposing a gentile mission.[4] But Paul based his authority on the appearance to him of the resurrected Christ commissioning him

to be an apostle to the Gentiles,[5] for this experience made everything else seem to him irrelevant.

It may come as a bit of a surprise, since Paul never heard Jesus,
to notice how much of Paul's teaching about the Christian
lifestyle actually echoes sayings of Jesus. Such sayings must have
been reported to him by Jesus' disciples or by those who had
learned them from disciples. After all, he may already have
learned what Jesus had to say in the process of persecuting his
disciples!

Actually, the sayings of Jesus at issue here are what has been
known down through history as the core of Jesus' teaching—what
we are familiar with under the title Sermon on the Mount.[6] This
is Matthew's enlargement of the Sermon in Q,[7] which is actually
not a speech Jesus ever made on a given occasion, but a very early
collection of his key sayings. Indeed, it may have been formulated
as a well-organized whole even before the Sayings Gospel Q itself
was composed.

Just how much this first collection of Jesus' sayings functioned
as a kind of "canon" of Jesus' teaching can be illustrated from what
may well be the oldest Christian document outside of the New
Testament, a manual of church order from around 100 C.E. Indeed, it was quoted as scripture by some church fathers. But then,
somewhat like the Sayings Gospel Q, subsequent texts that made
use of it in fact came to replace it. So it was completely lost, until
rediscovered in 1873, when it made a sensation comparable to that
of the discovery of the Dead Sea Scrolls and the Nag Hammadi
Codices. It is called the *Didache*, which in Greek means "Teaching"—the teaching of Jesus. The collection of sayings it contains is
familiar, since they are found in the Sermon on the Mount:

> There are two ways, one of life and one of death, and there
> is a great difference between these two ways. Now this is
> the way of life: First, "you shall love God, who made you";

second, "your neighbor as yourself"; and "whatever you do not wish to happen to you, do not do to another." The teaching of these words is this: "Bless those who curse you," and "pray for your enemies," and "fast for those who persecute you. For what credit is it, if you love those who loved you? Do not even the Gentiles do the same?" But "you must love those who hate you," and you will not have an enemy. Abstain from physical and bodily cravings. "If someone gives you a blow on your right cheek, turn to him the other as well," and you will be "perfect." If someone "forces you to go one mile, go with him two miles"; "if someone takes your cloak, give him your tunic also"; "if someone takes from you what belongs to you, do not demand it back," for you cannot do so. "Give to everyone who asks you, and do not demand it back," for the Father wants something from his own gifts to be given to everyone. Blessed is the one who gives according to the command, for such a person is innocent.[8]

The opening of the Sermon in Q reads:

Blessed are you poor, for God's reign is for you.
Blessed are you who hunger, for you will eat your fill.
Blessed are you who mourn, for you will be consoled.
Blessed are you when they insult and persecute you, and say
    every kind of evil against you because of the son of
    humanity. Be glad and exult, for vast is your reward in
    heaven. For this is how they persecuted the prophets who
    were before you.
Love your enemies and pray for those persecuting you.[9]

It is just such sayings of Jesus that his disciples were still using in Paul's time, and it is they that came to influence his own teaching about the Christian life.

Yet Paul did not explicitly ascribe this teaching to Jesus—in Paul's presentation, it stands in its own right:

> Bless those who persecute you; bless and do not curse them. Rejoice with those who rejoice, weep with those who weep. Live in harmony with one another; do not be haughty, but associate with the lowly; do not claim to be wiser than you are. Do not repay anyone evil for evil, but take thought for what is noble in the sight of all. If it is possible, so far as it depends on you, live peaceably with all. . . . Do not be overcome by evil, but overcome evil with good.
>
> See that none of you repays evil for evil, but always seek to do good to one another and to all.
>
> To the present hour we are hungry and thirsty, we are poorly clothed and beaten and homeless. . . . When reviled, we bless; when persecuted, we endure; when slandered, we speak kindly.[10]

Thus Paul actually advocated much the same way of life as did Jesus.

GOD'S VENGEANCE VERSUS GOD'S FORGIVENESS

Yet Paul was more learned in the scriptures than was Jesus, and so could quote Proverbs to strengthen the argument:

> If your enemies are hungry, feed them; if they are thirsty, give them something to drink . . .[11]

But Proverbs continues less charitably, and Paul goes along:

. . . for by doing this you will heap burning coals on their heads.[12]

This does not actually sound like loving one's enemies! Indeed, Paul could introduce this with another scriptural passage emphasizing God's retribution:

Vengeance is mine, I will repay, says the Lord.[13]

This is not the God that Jesus had discovered in the world of nature around him and had revealed to his disciples. Quite the reverse—Jesus spoke of a God who was impartial in his goodness to all, forgiving rather than revenging, loving even the bad and unjust:

Love your enemies and pray for those persecuting you, so that you may become sons of your Father, for he raises his sun on bad and good and rains on the just and unjust.[14]

So when Jesus wanted to explain God's kind handling of the bad and unjust, he told a parable about a wayward son who had gone astray, then remorsefully returned to his father, who received him with open arms:

But while he was still far off, his father saw him and was filled with compassion; he ran and put his arms around him and kissed him. Then the son said to him, "Father, I have sinned against heaven and before you; I am no longer worthy to be called your son." But the father said to his slaves, "Quickly, bring out a robe—the best one—and put it on him; put a ring on his finger and sandals on his feet. And get the fatted calf and kill it, and let us eat and celebrate; for this son of mine was dead and is alive again; he was lost and is found!" And they began to celebrate.[15]

What had happened to this central description of God by Jesus? After all, his revelation of who God really is had been celebrated as the most important thing he had to offer:

> At that time he said: I praise you, Father, Lord of heaven and earth, for you hid these things from sages and the learned, and disclosed them to children. Yes, Father, for that is what it has pleased you to do.
>
> Everything has been entrusted to me by my Father, and no one knows the Son except the Father, nor does anyone know the Father except the Son, and to whomever the Son chooses to reveal him.[16]

The revelation to Jesus of a Father in heaven who loves the bad as well as the good seems to have been lost from sight. What happened?

COPING WITH THIS EVIL GENERATION

Jesus' message of God reigning, which his disciples had resumed proclaiming after his death, did not create a mass movement within Judaism. Quite the contrary, the number of disciples decreased over the coming generation. Jesus' disciples actually underwent intra-Jewish persecution:

> When they bring you before synagogues, do not be anxious about how or what you are to say; for the holy Spirit will teach you in that hour what you are to say.

Blessed are you when they insult and persecute you, and say every kind of evil against you because of the son of humanity.[17]

It is not surprising that Jesus' disciples experienced other Jews of their time (not to speak of the impossible Gentiles) as "an evil generation."[18] As a result, "this generation" became a designation for those whom God rejects.[19] Woes were pronounced on their leaders, the Pharisees[20] and exegetes of the Law.[21] Thus, Jesus' sunny experience of God showering love on even the bad and unjust gave way to an overlay from the Old Testament of a God of justice obliged to punish sin.

PAUL'S LOVING BUT ANGRY GOD

It was much the same idea of a God whose justice requires retribution for sin that had already helped Paul make sense of Jesus' terrible end, crucifixion, the capital punishment administered by the Romans to the worst of criminals:

> . . . Christ Jesus, whom God put forward as a sacrifice of atonement by his blood.[22]

In Paul's thinking, the God of infinite love, still echoed in the traditions going back to Jesus, was combined with the scriptural traditions of the just God obliged to avenge evil. The result was the concept of a loving God sending his Son to placate a God wrathful over sin:

> But God proves his love for us in that while we still were sinners Christ died for us. Much more surely then, now that we have been justified by his blood, will we be saved through him from the wrath of God.[23]

Apparently the only way Paul could make sense of Jesus' terrible death on the cross was to think of a loving but angry God needing in this way to avenge humanity's disobedience. This is why Paul could focus his message so pointedly:

We proclaim Christ crucified.[24]

Paul's gospel was:

Christ died for our sins in accordance with the scriptures.[25]

PAUL'S OPPOSITION TO A JUDAIZING GOSPEL

Paul polemicized against what he called "Judaizing,"[26] by which he meant trying to superimpose on gentile Christians the precondition of having to conform to the Jewish lifestyle:

I am astonished that you are so quickly deserting the one who called you in the grace of Christ and are turning to a different gospel—not that there is another gospel, but there are some who are confusing you and want to pervert the gospel of Christ. But even if we or an angel from heaven should proclaim to you a gospel contrary to what we proclaimed to you, let that one be accursed! As we have said before, so now I repeat, if anyone proclaims to you a gospel contrary to what you received, let that one be accursed![27]

Paul reasoned that any such precondition to becoming a Christian, such as having to convert to Judaism, would produce a "both and" kind of salvation—you have to observe a good Jewish lifestyle *and* believe in Jesus—and that this would inevitably weaken the exclusive saving role of Jesus:

. . . so that the cross of Christ might not be emptied of its power.[28]

Those who favored gentile Christians adopting the Jewish lifestyle were no doubt less theoretical and more practical: Jesus' followers should walk in his footsteps (to use the modern idiom), and his walk of life was obviously Jewish. But Paul's lifestyle had been Jewish as well, yet for him this was not a prerequisite to salvation:

> To the Jews I became as a Jew, in order to win Jews. To those under the Law I became as one under the Law (though I myself am not under the Law) so that I might win those under the Law. To those outside the Law I became as one outside the Law (though I am not free from God's law but am under Christ's law) so that I might win those outside the Law. To the weak I became weak, so that I might win the weak. I have become all things to all people, that I might by all means save some. I do it all for the sake of the gospel, so that I might share in its blessings.[29]

Obviously Paul did not oppose Jesus' gospel itself, several of whose focal sayings he cited in his own message. Rather, he opposed requiring Gentiles to convert to Judaism.

THE GOSPEL OF JESUS

The completely new lifestyle Jesus developed for himself, and called upon others to practice as well, was not for his part meant as a means to appease an angry God in an effort to win his favor. Quite the reverse. It was because God was already active on all sides in a fatherly way that one could practice that lifestyle, for it consisted in receiving from God through the actions of others and God giving to others through one's own actions.

Thus Jesus' message was not a new law to which humans had to conform, not a morality laying out what they had to do to deserve God's favor. Rather, it was indeed *gospel,* good news, telling what God was doing for and through humans. Of course it was not Paul's gospel of "Christ crucified," but Jesus' own gospel of the kingdom of God: God reigning for and through people who listened to what Jesus had to say.

———•◆•———

WHERE DO WE GO FROM HERE?

First let me express appreciation to those of you who have gotten this far—you really are here! Not everybody made it—you are the hardy ones. But you can't spend the rest of your life on this page of the book. You have to move on. But where do you go from here?

Those of you who are with me here have come from very different places and will of course go in very different directions. Some of you are at home in the church to which you belong. But others of you are more restless and tend to move in one direction or the other. I want to speak especially to those of you who are less in the center than tending toward one end of the spectrum or the other.

THE SECULAR ALTERNATIVE

Let me first imagine those of you who have "outgrown" the usual church, the standard kind of Christianity you or your parents grew up in. You embrace humane causes and are a "good" person, but you do not need all this God-talk, much less the pomp and ceremony that seems to you more self-serving than pious—or more pious than sincere. Indeed, many of us have become secular, often without really realizing it, and do not want to return to what, for us at least, would now only be insincere.

I have tried in this little book to present Jesus as he really was, not as you and I may wish he had been. He lived in a culture that was uncritically religious (although of course, as we have shown at many places, he was critical of religious practices of his day and age). For him, God was simply a given. To present him as doing his thing without being related to God would be falsifying his reality. God-talk was the language he spoke, the reality in which he functioned.

Christians have tended to ascribe what Jesus did to who he was: the Son of God, the Christ, the Lord, and all that. But Jesus did not point to himself to understand what he was doing or to explain himself to others. He pointed to God: what he was doing was actually God reigning through human action. And so we must listen to his God-talk if we really want to take *him* seriously, to understand *him*.

God-talk is not empty talk. It can be and usually is one way of talking about reality, an important way built into religious cultures. God-talk is like a foreign language—it is just a way of talking about things that is different from the way we are used to. Someone who is speaking in a foreign language is not just saying nothing, but may be saying something very important, if only we could understand it. And when that foreign language does not even use the Latin alphabet, for example, Russian, Arabic, Chinese, or the Bible's own Hebrew and Greek, we may feel even more distanced. So we have to learn the alphabet and then the language to understand what the person is talking about. Many people are far enough out there in the secular world that they can no more understand God-talk than they can understand a foreign language they never studied.

Of course people can talk God-talk and be saying things that have no substance at all (just as they can use secular language to say nothing at all). But we must learn to translate God-talk before we know whether or not it is saying anything. Let me give a few oversimplified instances out of the past just to make you think.

Do angels have wings or not? When a Renaissance painter made a picture of an angel without wings that was supposed to be hung in a cathedral, the bishop of that cathedral rejected it with the blunt comment: "Did you ever see an angel without wings?" To this the painter replied: "Did you ever see an angel *with* wings?" The Renaissance painter seemed to be saying: "Angels are usually painted with wings, but angels themselves neither *do* nor *do not* have wings, since they are just part of our religious language that does not refer to something out there. So I can paint them however I want!"

Here the Renaissance painter and the more medieval bishop seem to have hit a basic disagreement about the existence of angels. But the real issue may lie elsewhere. What the bishop probably meant was only that the angel should be painted for the cathedral in the way that people are used to imagining angels, not in some newfangled Renaissance way that people would not like. If this was the disagreement, then we catch sight of an issue that can at least be debated. Perhaps you yourself would prefer angels on Christmas cards to have wings.

A recent book about Jesus has on its cover a picture of a young man without a beard. Frankly, I do not like the picture, though I am fully aware that we know absolutely nothing about how Jesus looked. I do know that the image of Jesus with a beard may come from sculptures of Socrates, with whom Jesus came to be identified, rather than from any memory about how Jesus looked. Still—and I must admit I prefer angels with wings—I guess I am just old-fashioned.

An even more empty debate about angels, it would seem at first glance, comes into view if we move back into the Dark Ages themselves: the medieval debate over how many angels can dance on the point of a needle! What kind of debate could have less substance to it? How could anyone take sides in such a debate, where both alternatives mean nothing?

But this reaction on our part is just because we do not understand late medieval culture—what was being debated was really a philosophical issue crucial at that time. Does everything have to have material substance, have size that fills space, in order to be real, or can things without material substance, such as principles, ideals, truths, be as real as sticks and stones? It was this philosophical issue that was being debated with this (to us) silly illustration of the dancing angels. So let me explain what the issue really was.

At that time angels were of course thought of as real. So if real things have to have material substance, that is, have to have size and fill space, then angels have to fill space in order to be real. No matter how minute that space may be, only so many could find room to dance on the point of a needle. So if you think that to be real, things must fill space, then you would answer the question by arguing that only a limited number of angels could dance on the point of a needle—if too many were dancing on the point of a needle, they would begin to push each other off!

But if you take the side of the philosophical debate that maintains that things without material substance are also real, then angels could be real and still not have material substance. In this case, an infinite number could dance on the point of a needle without pushing each other off, since none of them need have any "size" at all. So if you take the side of the argument that things can be real without having material substance, without having size that fills space, then you could reason that an infinite number of angels can dance on the point of a needle.

Philosophers today can still take that debate seriously as an important issue in the late Middle Ages leading up to the Renaissance, even though of course modern philosophers do not believe in the existence of angels with or without material substance. The moral of this story is: if you do not want to end up looking very superficial, you have to get into medieval culture far enough to see what they were really debating in their (to us) ridiculous terminology.

Still farther back in the early church, philosophically trained theologians debated over equally esoteric doctrines about Jesus, such as what kind of God or human he was, or what kind of both he was. So what language could we use about him that would get all that said just right?

What is surprising is that, in the metropolitan capitals of the various provinces of the Byzantine Empire (the Christendom of the day), the illiterate masses could get so aroused over those debates that there would be huge processions, even riots, with everybody shouting endlessly throughout the night the theological slogan of their patriarch. Yet these issues were so complicated and convoluted that, if I tried to lay them out in detail, it would no doubt just show how rusty I am on such dogmas of yesteryear, leaving you confused—or bored to death! After all, who cares? These are debates about which Christians of today have never heard and couldn't care less.

But why then did the illiterate masses get out in the streets to demonstrate? They certainly did not understand what was being debated, so how is it they got so aroused? Answer: they knew enough to know which side of the debate their patriarch had taken, and they weren't about to let some patriarch from another part of the Byzantine Empire tell them that their trusted leader was a heretic. No, they would stay loyal to their native son, who had begun among them and risen through the ranks up to the top, so they would not let him down! That was worth fighting for, which they did, when necessary. This may not be all that was at stake, but it certainly was a big part of it. After all, who wants those politicians back in Washington telling us what to do or think? Just imagine what a riot there would be if Congress told us which theological doctrines to believe!

These way-out illustrations, oversimplified as they may be, are intended to convince the most secular among you that God-talk is the language in which many substantive issues have been discussed down through the ages. Our rejection of them, indeed at times our ridicule, may be less evidence of our modern superiority than of our superficiality—our inability to understand what is brought to expression in any language other than our own.

Surely, even those of you who are more secular than religious have gotten this far in reading the book only because you have somehow sensed that Jesus, in spite of his God-talk, really had something to say. You must have heard something that rang a bell, something you thought you could understand, shining through his God-talk. Perhaps what got to you was the idea that everybody looking out for number one creates a vicious cycle from which no one escapes. Perhaps you got on board with the realization that God reigning is in reality merely what others do for you and what is done for others through you. Whatever it was that clicked with you to keep you reading until this concluding chapter, I hope to put into focus for you by summarizing what Jesus' gospel really was, and what your gospel could be from now on.

THE EVANGELICAL ALTERNATIVE

Let me now turn to those of you who have long since decided to commit yourself to Christianity, to take it seriously—you who do not want to let your Christian experience boil down to just going through the motions of the traditional church service. You want to take your faith to heart, to feel it and live it as best you can.

You have read the book hoping that it would help you in your Christian commitment. And I surely hope it has! But no doubt you too have questions about where you are to go from here. So let me try to bring some of them to expression, so we can talk about them.

It may well seem to you that the gospel of Jesus did not include all that is high and holy in the Christian gospel as we know it. All those magnificent, transcendent, Christian beliefs seem absent from the original gospel of Jesus—his "gospel" may seem minimal by comparison with *the* gospel! Missing from his gospel are not only where he came from ("conceived by the Holy Spirit, born of the Virgin Mary"), but also what he came to do. Where, after all, is "the saving work of Christ": dying for our sins, rising on the third day, appearing to the apostles resurrected from the dead? These are, after all, the gospel *about* Jesus, which you, understandably enough, believe and cherish. But if you really are committed to Jesus, then you should be committed to the gospel *of* Jesus, which is what I have written this book to try to help you see and understand: the "good news" Jesus offered people during his public ministry.

But when you turn to the public ministry of Jesus, the most dramatic stories *about* Jesus were not included in the presentation of the gospel *of* Jesus! Perhaps the most dramatic passage in all the Gospels is his feeding "five thousand men, besides women and children," using "five loaves and two fish," with "twelve baskets full of the broken pieces" left over.[1] This is followed immediately by the story of Jesus walking on the water: the terrified disciples are in a boat on the Sea of Galilee during a storm; Jesus comes to them, "walking on the sea"; Peter attempts to do the same but must be rescued by Jesus; and when Jesus gets into the boat, the wind ceases.[2] When I ask devout Christians what they make of such stories as these, the usual reply is that they don't take them literally. But if I press my question by asking, "Then how do you take them?" I tend to get a painful silence. So let me try to answer my own question.

These stories, blown all out of proportion though they are, give the true impression Jesus made on those who experienced the gospel he preached and practiced. He was there for them and did all he could to help them in whatever plight he found them in. He turned the other cheek.[3] He gave the shirt off his back.[4] He went the second mile.[5] He gave, asking for nothing back.[6] He lent to those who could not reciprocate.[7] In sum, he pitied those in need[8] and acted accordingly.

Jesus applied the Golden Rule to everyone: treat everyone the way you want to be treated![9] It was not just his neighbor whom he loved.[10] He loved those who would not love him in return.[11] He explained that loving your neighbor even means loving the ethnic group you have been taught to despise. His example was a Samaritan—Jews were of course in agreement that there was no such thing as a "good" Samaritan! But Jesus told the story of a Samaritan who took care of a Jew who had fallen among thieves, whose plight had been ignored by "good" Jews, who had left him in the gutter "half dead."[12] The Samaritan had responded to the Jew's situation out of pity for the plight of a fellow human. That is, you must even love your enemy.[13]

Jesus derived the love of enemies from God, and so revealed God in a new way. You are to be full of pity, "just as your Father is full of pity."[14] You are to love your enemies and pray for those persecuting you, "so that you may become sons of your Father, for he raises his sun on bad and good and rains on the just and unjust."[15] It is the reigning of this Father that frees you from having to look out for number one; you can live as free from anxiety as the birds of the air and the lilies of the field, for they do nothing to care for themselves and yet receive from God their food and clothing, just as you can.[16] You are to pray to God to reign for you ("Thy kingdom come"), which he put quite concretely: "Our day's bread give us today."[17] And you can trust God that it will happen:

> If you, though evil, know how to give good gifts to your children, by how much more will the Father from heaven give good things to those who ask him![18]

Jesus preached this as a new revelation of God.[19] Should we not pay attention to Jesus' revelation of God?

Just as the Gospels present Jesus performing miracles all out of proportion to reality, which nonetheless derive from the real impact of what Jesus in fact actually did for people in their lives, just so the Gospels present Jesus predicting his death in so much detail that such predictions have long since been recognized as merely summaries of Mark's passion narrative with which his Gospel concludes.[20] But Jesus of course realized that his not looking out for number one, in the radical sense in which he implemented this ideal, could not fail to put his life daily at risk. Furthermore, his proclaiming that what he was doing was just letting God reign could not fail to sound dangerous to the Roman army of occupation.

Herod Antipas, tetrarch of Galilee, was the vassal ruler of the area where Jesus set up his base camp, in Capernaum. But during Jesus' public ministry it was this same Herod Antipas who had John the Baptist beheaded! In such crises, Jesus, by crossing over the frontier into the territory of Herod Philip, could reach a safer haven, Bethsaida, which was also on the northern shore of the Sea of Galilee just next to Capernaum. But Jesus, by leaving Galilee to go to Jerusalem for Passover, when tensions with the Romans were always high, was surely throwing caution to the winds. Given the high profile he had by then, only augmented by his confrontations with the establishment during that holy week, the inevitable happened. He might well have escaped, as the scene in the garden of Gethsemane suggests, but he did not.[21] He would stand by his word, come what may. And it came.

WHERE DO WE GO FROM HERE?

You may prefer to stay where you have been all along, a modern secular person of good intentions, a committed evangelical Christian believing the gospel about Jesus, or someone somewhere in between. But if you just stand pat where you have been this far, the gospel of Jesus will haunt you—it won't give you peace until you come to grips with it. So come to grips with it, now, before you put this little book to one side. Listen to what Jesus had to say, hear his gospel, and let it change your life for good. This is why I wrote this book, for you. Take it and use it, for yourself.

NOTES

CHAPTER ONE: THE LOST
GOSPEL OF JESUS

1. Mark 13:2, 14.
2. Q 3:7–9, 16b–17 = Matt.
   3:7–10, 11–12 = Luke 3:7–9,
   16b–17
3. Q 4:1–4, 9–12, 5–8, 13 = Matt.
   4:1–11 = Luke 4:1–4, 9–12, 5–8,
   13.
4. Matt. 5–7.
5. Luke 6.20–49.
6. *Gospel of Thomas* (Nag Hammadi
   Codex II, Tractate 2).
7. Oxyrhynchus Papyri 1, 654, and
   655.
8. Mark 13:10.
9. Mark 7:3–4.
10. Mark 5:41; 7:34; 15:34.
11. Mark 7:31.
12. Q 6:34; 12:29–30.
13. Q 7:1–9.
14. Q 11:14–15.
15. Q 7:22.
16. Q 10:13.
17. Q 10:9.
18. Q 10:9.
19. Q 11:20.
20. Q 11:2b–3.

21. Q 11:11–13.
22. Q 12:22b, 24, 29–31.
23. Q 10:7–9.
24. Q 7:34.
25. Mark 6:32–44; 8:1–10; John
    6:1–15.
26. Acts 12:25.
27. Luke 22:30.
28. Luke 4.13.
29. Luke 22:3, 31.
30. Luke 22:35–38.
31. Mark 14:43.
32. Mark 14:47.
33. Q 10:4.
34. Acts 1:8.
35. Acts 9:31.
36. Gal. 2:9.
37. Q 7:31–34; 10:10–15; 11:29–30.
38. Q 13:34–35.
39. Rom. 15:26.
40. Q 6:20.
41. Q 7:22.
42. Acts 11:26.
43. Mark 14:67; Matt. 2:23.
44. Acts 24:5.
45. Matt. 10:5–6, 23.
46. Acts 1:8; 8:4–25.
47. Matt. 28:18–20.

48. Matt. 5–7.
49. Luke 6:20–49.
50. Q 11:2b–4; Matt. 6:9–13.
51. Q 11:9–13; Matt. 7:7–11.
52. Q 12:22b–31; Matt. 6:25–33.

CHAPTER THREE: JESUS WAS
A GALILEAN JEW

1. Matt. 26:73.
2. Matt. 16:17.
3. John 1:42.
4. John 21:15–17.
5. Mark 10:46.
6. Acts 4:36.
7. Acts 13:6.
8. Acts 1:23.
9. Acts 15:22.
10. Mark 15:11; John 18:40.
11. Mark 3:18; Acts 1:13.
12. Mark 3:18; Acts 1:13.
13. Luke 6:15; Acts 1:13.
14. Mark 3:17.
15. Mark 7:33–34.
16. Matt. 15:30.
17. Mark 5:41.
18. Luke 8:54.
19. Acts 9:36, 40.
20. Mark 14:36.
21. Matt. 26:39; Luke 22:41–42.
22. Q 10:5.
23. Luke 24:36; John 20:19, 21, 26.
24. Matt. 6:9–13; Luke 11:2–4.
25. Rom. 8:15b–16.
26. Gal. 4:6.
27. 1 Cor. 16:22.
28. Rev. 22:20.
29. *Didache* 10:6.
30. Mark 11:9; Matt. 21:9, 15; John 12:13.
31. Ps. 118:25–26.
32. Luke 19:38.
33. Rev. 19:1–7.

34. Mark 15:34; Matt. 27:46.
35. Mark 10:51.
36. John 20:16.
37. John 1:38.
38. John 20:16.
39. Mark 10:51.
40. Matt. 9:28; 20:33; Luke 18:41.
41. Mark 9:5.
42. Matt. 17:4; Luke 9:33.
43. Mark 11:21.
44. Matt. 21:20.
45. Mark 14:45.
46. Matt. 26:49.
47. Luke 22:47.
48. Matt. 26:25.
49. Matt. 23:7.
50. Matt. 23:8.
51. Q 6:46.
52. Matt. 26:25, 49; Mark 9:5; 11:21; 14:45.
53. John 1:38, 49; 3:2; 4:31; 6:25; 9:2; 11:8.
54. John 3:26.
55. Matt. 2:23; Luke 1:26; 2:4, 39; 4:29.
56. Acts 26:26.
57. Q 12:27.
58. 1 Kings 10; 2 Chron. 9.
59. John 8:6.
60. After John 7:36, or 7:52, or 21:25, or Luke 21:38.
61. John 7:53–8:11.
62. Q 6:35.
63. Q 6:41–42.
64. Q 6:43–44.
65. Q 6:47–49.
66. Q 7:24.
67. Q 10:3.
68. Q 10:11.
69. Q 11:33.
70. Q 12:6.
71. Q 12:7.

72. Q 12:24, 27.
73. Q 12:28.
74. Q 12:54–55.
75. Q 13:18–19, 20–21.
76. Q 14:34–35.
77. Q 15:4–5a, 7.
78. Q 17:23–24.
79. Q 17:37.
80. Q 10:21.
81. Mark 2:23–28.
82. Mark 10:4; Deut. 24:1–4.
83. Mark 10:6–7; Gen. 1:27; 2:24.
84. Mark 10:11–12.
85. Q 16:18.
86. Mark 12:1–9.
87. Mark 12:10–11; Ps. 118:22–23; Acts 4:11; 1 Pet. 2:7.
88. *Gospel of Thomas* (Nag Hammadi Codex II, Tractate 2), saying 65.
89. Luke 1–2.
90. Luke 2:41–52.
91. Mark 12:28–34; Matt. 22:34–40; Luke 10:25–28.
92. Luke 10:29–35.
93. Luke 10:36–37.
94. Lev. 19:15–18.
95. Q 6:27–28, 35c–d.
96. Luke 4:16–30.
97. Isa. 61:1–2.
98. Matt. 5:21–48.
99. Matt. 5:32, see Q 16:18 and Mark 10:11–12; Matt. 5:39–42, see Q 6:29–30; Matt. 5:44–47, see Q 6:27–28, 32–35.
100. Q 10:21.
101. Luke 2:41–52.
102. John 7:14–16.
103. William Shakespeare, *As You Like It*, act 2, scene 1.
104. In Nag Hammadi tractates: *Gospel of Thomas* (Codex II, Tractate 2), saying 12; *(First)*

Apocalypse of James (V, 3), 32,2–3; 43,19; *(Second) Apocalypse of James* (V, 4), e.g., 44,13–14,18; 60,12–13; 61,14.
105. Mark 2:15–17.
106. Q 7:1–9; John 4:46b–54.
107. Q 7:3.
108. Matt. 8:7.
109. Luke 7:5.
110. Acts 10.
111. Mark 7:26.
112. Matt. 15:22.
113. Mark 7:27.
114. Mark 7:29–30.
115. Matt. 7:6.
116. John 12:21–22.
117. Matt. 4:23; 9:35; Luke 4:15.
118. Mark 1:39.
119. Luke 4:44.
120. Mark 1:21–27.
121. Luke 4:16–30.
122. Mark 3:1–6.
123. John 6:59.
124. John 18:20.
125. Q 6:34; 12:29–30.
126. Matt. 5:47; 6:7–8a; 18:17.
127. Matt. 10:5–6, 23.
128. Q 11:39b–48.
129. Q 11:49–51.
130. Q 10:13–15.
131. Q 13:34–35.
132. Acts 4:36–37.
133. Acts 11:19–26.
134. Gal. 2:1–3.
135. Gal. 2:1–10.
136. 1 Cor. 9:20–21.
137. Gal. 5:14.
138. Mark 12:28–34; Matt. 22:34–40; Luke 10:25–28.
139. Luke 10:29b.
140. Lev. 19:15c–18.
141. Luke 10:30–37.

142. Luke 10:30–37.
143. Q 7:1–9.
144. Mark 7:24–30.
145. Gal. 2:12.
146. Acts 10:1–48.
147. Acts 11:1–18.
148. Gal. 2:11–21.
149. Acts 15:36–40.
150. Gal. 2:10.
151. Mark 1:16–20.
152. Acts 18:3.
153. Gal. 2:15.
154. Gal. 5:3.
155. Gal. 5:6.
156. Luke 15:11–32.
157. Gal. 1:4.
158. 1 Cor. 2:2.
159. 1 Cor. 1:13.

CHAPTER FOUR: WHAT WE DO AND DO NOT KNOW ABOUT JESUS

1. Q 4:16.
2. Mark 6:3.
3. John 7:5.
4. Mark 3:21.
5. Mark 3:31–35.
6. Mark 6:4.
7. John 2:1–11.
8. John 2:4.
9. John 19:25.
10. John 19:26–27.
11. Acts 1:14.
12. 1 Cor. 15:7.
13. Gal. 1:18–19.
14. 1 Cor. 9:5.
15. *Gospel of Thomas* (Nag Hammadi Codex II, Tractate 2), saying 12.
16. *Gospel of Thomas*, saying 13.
17. *Apocryphon of James* (Nag Hammadi Codex I, Tractate 2); *(First) Apocalypse of James* (V, 3); *(Second) Apocalypse of James* (V, 4).
18. *Gospel of Thomas* (Nag Hammadi Codex II, Tractate 2); *Book of Thomas* (II, 7).
19. *Book of Thomas*, 138,4–20.
20. Luke 2:42; 3:23.
21. Matt. 2:1.
22. Luke 8:2.
23. Luke 7:38.
24. John 12:3; 11:2.
25. Matt. 8:28.
26. Matt. 4:13 = Luke 4:16 = Q 4:16.
27. Mark 1:24; 10:47; 14:67; 16:6; Luke 24:19.
28. Luke 8:3.
29. Mark 15:40.
30. John 19:25.
31. Acts 12:12.
32. Luke 8:3.
33. Luke 8:3; Mark 15:40; 16:1.
34. Matt. 27:56 parallel to Mark 15:40.
35. Mark 5:3.
36. Mark 5:18.
37. Mark 5:19.
38. Luke 8:3.
39. Luke 8:3; Mark 15:41.
40. Mark 15:40–41; John 19:25.
41. Mark 14:67, 69, 70.
42. Mark 14:29–31.
43. Mark 15:47.
44. Mark 16:1.
45. Mark 16:5.
46. Matt. 28:2.
47. Luke 24:4.
48. Mark 16:7.
49. Mark 16:8.
50. Luke 24:10–11.
51. John 20:1.
52. John 20:2–10.
53. John 20:11–18.
54. Mark 16:9.
55. Mark 15:24.
56. Ps. 22:18.

57. Mark 3:21.
58. Mark 3:31.
59. Mark 3:34–35.
60. Q 7:59–60.
61. Q 12:53.
62. Q 14:26.
63. Luke 14:26.
64. *Gospel of Philip* (Nag Hammadi Codex II, Tractate 3), 59,6–11.
65. *Gospel of Philip,* 65,20; 70,19; 76,7; 82,1.
66. *Gospel of Philip,* 58,26–59,6.
67. *Gospel of Philip,* 63,30–64,9.
68. *Gospel of Philip,* 58,33–34.
69. *Pistis Sophia,* 125,4–5.
70. *(Second) Apocalypse of James* (Nag Hammadi Codex V, Tractate 4), 56,14–20.
71. Mark 12:25.
72. *Gospel of Mary* (Berlin Codex 8502, Tractate 1), 10,1–6.
73. *Gospel of Mary,* 17,7–18,15.
74. Rom. 16.
75. Rom. 16:16.
76. 1 Thess. 5:26.
77. 1 Cor. 16:20; 2 Cor. 13:12.
78. 1 Pet. 5:14.
79. Mark 2:20.
80. Eph. 5:32; Rev. 21:2, 9; 22:17

CHAPTER FIVE: JESUS WAS CONVERTED BY JOHN
1. Luke 3:23.
2. Mark 1.6, Q 7.33.
3. Q 7:24–26.
4. Q 7:29–30.
5. John 1:28.
6. Q 10:4.
7. Mark 1:12–13; Q 4:1–13.
8. Luke 3:11.
9. John 1:43.
10. Mark 6:1–6a; Luke 4:16–30.
11. Mark 6:4.

12. Mark 1:21; Q 4:16; Matt. 4:13.
13. John 3:22; 4:1.
14. John 4:2.
15. *Testimony of Truth* (Nag Hammadi Codex IX, Tractate 3), 69,15–17.
16. Gal. 2:15.
17. 1 Cor. 1:17a.
18. Matt. 28:19.
19. Acts 19:1–7.
20. Mark 1:10.
21. John 1:29–34.
22. Mark 2:18–20.
23. Luke 11:1–4.
24. Q 3:7–9.
25. Q 3:9.
26. Q 3:16b.
27. Q 3:17.
28. Q 3:9.
29. Q 6:43–45.
30. Luke 13:6–9.
31. Mark 11:12–14.
32. Matt. 21:18–19.
33. Q 6:27–28, 35c–d, 29–30
34. Q 11:29.
35. Q 7:31; 11:29, 30, 31, 32, 50, 51.
36. Q 11:39b–44.
37. Q 11:46b–48, 52.
38. Q 11:49–51, 13.34–35.
39. Q 13:28
40. Q 10:21.
41. Q 3:16b–17.
42. Q 11:20.
43. Q 7:18–19, 22–23.
44. Q 17:24.
45. Q 13:35.
46. Ps. 118:26a.
47. Mark 11:9.
48. Q 3:16b.
49. Mark 1:10.
50. Acts 2:2–4.
51. John 1:29, 34, 36; 3:28.
52. Q 3:7–9, 16b–17.
53. Q 3:21b.

54. Q 7:18–35.
55. Q 7:26–28, citing Mal. 3:1.
56. Q 7:29–30.
57. Q 7:33–34.
58. Q 7:35.
59. Q 7:28.
60. Q 3:16b.
61. Luke 3:19–21.
62. Acts 13:23–25.
63. Matt. 3:14–15.
64. Q 7:19.
65. Isa. 61:1 in Greek.
66. Q 7:22.
67. Q 3–7.
68. Q 3:16b–17.
69. Q 7:18–19.
70. Q 7:22.
71. Q 3:21b–22.
72. Q 6:20.
73. Q 7:1–9.
74. Q 7:24.
75. Q 7:23.
76. Q 7:1–9.
77. Q 7:6b–8.
78. Q 6:20–49.
79. Luke 7:21.
80. Luke 7:11–17.
81. Mark 3:13.
82. Q 11:14.
83. Matt. 12:22.
84. Matt. 9:32–34.
85. Mark 10:46–52.
86. Matt. 20:29–34.
87. Matt. 9:27–31.
88. Mark 1:40–45 used in Matt. 8:1–4, and Mark 2:1–12 used in Matt. 9:1–8.
89. Mark 5:21–43.
90. Mark 5:42.
91. Mark 5:23.
92. Matt. 9:18.
93. Mark 5:39.
94. Matt. 11:4.
95. Matt. 11:2.
96. Matt. 11:19.
97. John 10:25, 32, 33, 37, 38.
98. John 10:40–42.
99. Q 3:16b; Acts 19:6.
100. Q 7:28.
101. Q 10:22.
102. Mark 6:17–29.
103. Matt. 14:3–12.
104. Matt. 14:12–13.
105. Mark 6:30–31.
106. Q 7:24.
107. Matt. 11:28.
108. Matt. 3–11.
109. Q 7:22.
110. Q 7:23.
111. Q 7:24.
112. Matt. 11:2.
113. Matt. 12–28.
114. Matt. 10:5–6, 23.
115. Matt. 28:20.
116. Q 16:16.
117. Matt. 1–2; Luke 1–2.
118. Acts 1:21–22.
119. John 1:40.
120. Acts 10:37.
121. Acts 13:24.
122. Acts 18:24–19:7.
123. Acts 18:25.
124. Acts 19:6.

CHAPTER SIX: JESUS' LIFESTYLE UNDERWRITTEN BY GOD HIMSELF

1. Q 6:46–49.
2. Q 10:3–12, 16.
3. Mark 6:7–13.
4. Matt. 10:1, 5–42.
5. Q 10:5–6, 10–11.
6. Matt. 10:11.
7. Q 10:7.

8. *Didache* 11:3–6.
9. Matt. 10:10b.
10. Matt. 10:8b.
11. Q 10:4.
12. Matt. 10:9.
13. Luke 9:1–6.
14. Luke 10:1–16.
15. I Cor. 9:1–6, 12.
16. Acts 27:1–28:13.
17. Rom. 15:26.
18. Acts 18:3.
19. Luke 10:4–11.
20. Acts 2:44–45; 4:32–35.
21. Acts 4:37.
22. Acts 5:1–2.
23. Matt. 10:5–6, 23.
24. Matt. 28:18–20.
25. Q 10:4–11.
26. Luke 22:30.
27. Luke 22:35–38.
28. Mark 14:47.
29. Q 6:20; 7:28; 10:9; 11:2b, 20, 52; 12:31; 13:18, 20, 28; 16:16; 17:20, 21.
30. Q 6:20; 7:22; 12:28–29.
31. Q 6:21; 10:7, 8; 11:3, 11–12; 12:24, 29; 13:29, 28.
32. Q 10:9.
33. Q 6:29, 29´30/Matt. 5:41, 30.
34. Q 6:27–28, 35c–d.
35. Q 11:14, 20.
36. Q 4:13; 11:21–22.
37. Q 6:43–49.
38. Luke 3:10–14.
39. Q 6:29.
40. Q 10:4.
41. Q 3:16b; Mark 1:7.
42. Q 10:4.
43. Q 10:4.
44. Q 11:2b–3.
45. Q 10:4; Matt. 10:10.
46. Q 6:29, 29´30/Matt. 5:41, 30.
47. Q 12:24, 27.

48. Q 12:29–31.
49. Q 4:16; 7:1.
50. Mark 4:37–39.
51. John 21:3–13.
52. Luke 5:1–11.
53. Q 7:1–9; John 4:46–54.
54. John 1:40.
55. John 1:40–44.
56. Mark 1:16–18.
57. Mark 1:20.
58. Mark 1:29–31.
59. Mark 2:1.
60. Mark 3:21.
61. Mark 3:31, 33–34.
62. Q 14:26.
63. Q 12:53.
64. Q 10:2.
65. Q 9:59–60.
66. Q 12:31.
67. Q 12:24, 27, 29–31.
68. Q 10:4.
69. Q 7:33–34.
70. Q 10:7–8.
71. Q 10:9.
72. Q 10:5.
73. Q 11:20.
74. Q 11:2b–3.
75. Q 12:24.
76. Q 12:31.

CHAPTER SEVEN: JESUS'
TRUST IN GOD

1. Gen. 6:5–8:9.
2. Gen. 9:8–17.
3. Gen. 19:24; Rev. 14:10.
4. Ps. 11:6.
5. I Kings 18:24.
6. I Kings 18:38–39.
7. Q 12:6–7.
8. Q 12:22b–31.
9. *Gospel of Thomas* (Oxyrhynchus Papyrus 655), saying 36.

10. Q 6:27–28, 35c–d, 29, 29´30/Matt. 5:41, 30.
11. Matt. 5:43–44.
12. Matt. 14:26–32.
13. Mark 6:45–51.
14. Matt. 14:15–21.
15. Q 10:13.
16. John 4:48.
17. Q 11:15; see Mark 3:22.
18. 2 Kings 1:2–16.
19. Mark 13:22.
20. Q 11:20.
21. Exod. 20:7.
22. Q 11:2b.
23. Luke 15:18.
24. Exod. 6:3.
25. Matt. 6:10.
26. Luke 11:2b.
27. Q 11:2b–4.
28. Matt. 6:13.
29. Q 11:9–13.
30. Q 11:20.
31. Mark 9:17–18, 20, 22.
32. Mark 9:26–27.
33. Q 10:8–9.
34. Q 7:28.
35. Q 11:52.
36. Q 11:46b.
37. Q 16:16.
38. Q 13:18–19.
39. Q 13:20–21.
40. Q 17:20–21.
41. Q 12:31.
42. Q 12:29.
43. Q 7:22.
44. Q 6:20–21.
45. Q 10:7–8.
46. Q 10:9.
47. Q 11:4.
48. Q 6:30.
49. Matt. 18:23–35.
50. Q 6:32, 34.

51. Q 17:3–4.
52. Q 6:36–38.
53. Q 6:31.
54. Q 6:27–28, 35c–d.
55. Matt. 5:43.
56. Q 6:29, 29´30/Matt. 5:41, 30.

CHAPTER EIGHT: JESUS' VIEW OF HIMSELF
1. Mic. 5:2, quoted Matt. 2:6.
2. 1 Sam. 16:1–13; 17:12.
3. Luke 2:1–7.
4. Isa. 7:14, quoted Matt. 1:23.
5. Matt. 1–2.
6. Luke 1–2.
7. Mark 1:11.
8. Ps. 2:7, in Luke 3:22.
9. Matt. 1:18.
10. Luke 1:35.
11. John 1:1.
12. Q 4:3, 9.
13. Q 4:5–7.
14. Q 10:22.
15. Q 6:27–28, 35c–d; see also Matt. 5:44–45.
16. Q 6:36; 11:2b, 13; 12:30.
17. Song of Sol. 1:5; 2:7; 3:5, 10; 5:8, 16; 8:4.
18. Q 10:6.
19. Ps. 8:4.
20. E.g., Ezek. 2:1; 3:1; 4:1.
21. Dan. 7:13.
22. Dan. 7:1–14.
23. *Gospel of Thomas* (Nag Hammadi Codex II, Tractate 2), saying 76.
24. Q 9:58.
25. Q 9:57–60.
26. Q 12:10.
27. Q 7:34.
28. Q 6:22.
29. Q 11:30.
30. Q 12:8–9.

31. 1 Kings 10:1–10, 13; 2 Chron. 9:1–9, 12.
32. Jon. 3.
33. Q 11:31–32.
34. Q 12:40.
35. Q 17:24, 26–27, 30.
36. Mark 13:26–27.
37. Matt. 24:30–31.
38. Dan. 7:13–14.
39. Matt. 25:31–32.
40. Q 11:19.
41. Q 22:28, 30.
42. Matt. 19:28.
43. Q 11:49–51; 13:34–35.
44. Luke 11:49.
45. Matt. 23:34.
46. Q 7:33–35.
47. Q 7:19.
48. Q 7:22.
49. Q 13:35.
50. Ps. 118:26a.
51. Mark 11:9.
52. Matt. 21:9; Luke 19:38; John 12:13.
53. Mark 1:7.
54. Matt. 3:11.
55. John 1:27.
56. Acts 19:4.
57. John 6:48, 8.12, 10:9, 11; 14:6.
58. Q 11:15.
59. Q 11:20.
60. Q 11:19.
61. Q 12:30b.
62. Q 12:31.
63. Q 10:8–9a.
64. Q 10:9b.
65. Q 11:2b–3.
66. John 8:28.
67. Q 13:35.
68. 1 Cor. 2:2.
69. Mark 10:45.
70. Q 16:16.

71. Mark 8:31; 9:31; 10:33–34.

CHAPTER NINE: THE END AS THE BEGINNING

1. Mark 15:34.
2. Mark 15:37.
3. Luke 23:46.
4. John 19:30.
5. Q 6:36.
6. Q 12:6–7.
7. Q 11:11–13.
8. Q 12:22b, 28–29, 30b–31.
9. John 19:28.
10. Mark 1:17.
11. John 21:3; Luke 5:3.
12. Q 12:3–4.
13. 1 Cor. 15:3–8.
14. Acts 9:1–9; 22:5–11; 26:12–18.
15. John 20:14–18.
16. Luke 24:13–35.
17. John 20:24–29.

CHAPTER TEN: THE GOSPEL OF JESUS AND THE GOSPEL OF PAUL

1. Gal. 1:15–2:14.
2. Phil. 3:6.
3. 2 Cor. 5:16–17.
4. Matt. 10:5–6, 23.
5. 1 Cor. 15:8; Gal. 1:11–16.
6. Matt. 5–7.
7. Q 6.20–49.
8. *Didache* 1.
9. Q 6:20–23, 27–28.
10. Rom. 12:14–18, 21; 1 Thess. 5:15; 1 Cor. 4:11–13.
11. Rom. 12.20a, Prov. 25.21.
12. Rom. 12:20b; Prov. 25:22.
13. Rom. 12:19; Deut. 32:35.
14. Q 6:27–28, 35c–d.
15. Luke 15:20–24.
16. Q 10:21–22.

17. Q 12:11–12; 6:22.
18. Q 11:29.
19. Q 7:31; 11:29, 30, 31, 32, 50, 51.
20. Q 11:39b–44.
21. Q 11:46b–48, 52.
22. Rom. 3:24–25.
23. Rom. 5:8–9.
24. 1 Cor. 1:23.
25. 1 Cor. 15:3.
26. Gal. 2:14.
27. Gal. 1:6–9.
28. 1 Cor. 1:17.
29. 1 Cor. 9:20–23.

EPILOGUE
1. Matt. 14:13–21.
2. Matt. 14:22–33.
3. Q 6:29a.
4. Q 6:29b.
5. Q 6:29´30/Matt. 5:41.
6. Q 6:30.
7. Q 6:34.
8. Q 6:36.
9. Q 6:31.
10. Mark 12:31.
11. Q 6:32.
12. Luke 10:29–37.
13. Q 6:27.
14. Q 6:36.
15. Q 6:27–28, 35c–d.
16. Q 12:22b–31.
17. Q 11:2b–3.
18. Q 11:13.
19. Q 10:21–22.
20. Mark 8:31; 9:31; 10:33–34.
21. Mark 14:32–42.